THE LEAD

MAP

Your Path to Becoming an Exceptional Leader

Bruce M. Anderson

Judith M. O'Connor

This book is published by Thinking Partners, Inc., a leadership coaching company. We provide coaching services to leaders in both publicly and privately held businesses throughout the United States. Our services include:

- Leadership Coaching
- Team Development
- Leadership Training

www.thinkingpartners.com

To buy additional copies of this book, visit our website.

Third Edition

The Leadership Mastery Map®

Copyright © 2013

Bruce M. Anderson
Judith M. O'Connor

All rights reserved.

Table of Contents

Exceptional Leaders

Exceptional Leaders

Introduction

THIS BOOK WILL HELP YOU navigate today's fast-paced business environment. Its useful content will assist in your ongoing exploration of the skills necessary in becoming an exceptional leader. It is designed for busy, successful people who are immersed in business today, and who are already functioning as leaders.

As leadership coaches, we have had the privilege of observing and coaching many leaders over the last 20 years. We know that leaders want to be exceptional at what they do. And, we have discovered a number of things that exceptional leaders should do and should *not* do in order to contribute significant value to the performance of their organization.

We have learned that focusing on a list of "top ten things" that you must do as a leader is not sufficient. It is not that simple. There are literally hundreds of things that leaders must attend to in order to be effective. Each varies in importance within the organization depending upon unique situations and demands.

We know that there are hundreds of books about leadership. This book is a concise overview of some of the key concepts of leadership. It is practical and is ground in the fundamentals. You can browse through it periodically to see how you are doing. And you can use it for deeper self-assessment and learning. Our clients keep it as a ready reference for self-evaluation and for evaluating others. You can take an on-line Leadership Mastery Map assessment at www.leadershipmasterymap.com.

We are using The Leadership Mastery Map® to provide a context for the work of the leader. The map will help you explore the territory of leadership. Whether you are a newly appointed leader, a small business owner, or a senior executive in a large corporation, you can use this book to uncover hundreds of practical ideas and thought-provoking insights about leadership.

The Leadership Mastery Map® is a representation of the *four quadrant model* developed by Ken Wilber. We have adapted Ken's model to provide a concise, yet complete map for decision making and thinking about leadership. Topics are categorized based on the model.

To fully explore this insightful way of viewing the world, visit Ken's website at www.integralinstitute.com, and read his book, *A Theory of Everything: An Integral Vision for Business, Politics, Science and Spirituality* [1]

We welcome your comments. Please contact us at bruce@thinkingpartners.com

Bruce M. Anderson, MBA, Master Certified Coach

Judith M. O'Connor, M. Ed, Master Certified Coach

See our websites at:

www.thinkingpartners.com

www.leadershipmasterymap.com

Applying the Concepts in This Book

THERE ARE A NUMBER OF APPROACHES that you can use in learning to apply the concepts in this book.

Self-Assessments

We have found that the most effective learning occurs with interaction between the learner and the material. Just reading the material may spark some new thinking. However, making notes, doing a self-assessment, and prioritizing the topics that are important to you, will all increase the likelihood that you will recall and apply the information when it is needed.

Take the On-Line Assessment

Go to www.leadershipmasterymap.com.

Ratings of Each Topic

After reading each topic, score it according to its current importance in your job and the culture of your organization.

Importance in my work (scale of 1–5)

1. Not applicable to my job
2. Marginally applicable to my work
3. Nice to be able to do this well
4. It is very important that I do this well
5. Critical to my success. I must have mastery of this.

Creating a Development Plan

"After all our learning, we only acquire what we put into practice.". . . Goethe

After reading the individual topic areas and determining the relevancy in your job and your proficiency, the next step is to prioritize improvement areas. For each topic there is a place for you to write those "next actions" prompted by reading the material.

Ultimately you will want to select the top five or so topic areas that you will focus on for your development.

Use for Staff Meetings

Some of our clients use this material during staff meetings. They reserve time to cover a topic that strikes them as important to their current situation. They discuss how each staff member is performing in that area and ways to support each other and the organization in implementing desired change. Other clients rotate through the table of contents, thus allowing for conversations in all four quadrants of the Map.

Curriculum for Leadership Programs

This book can be a very useful tool for assessing and conducting A training needs assessment for a leadership group. A customized curriculum can be developed to address a group's specific needs. The Leadership Mastery Map On-Line Assessment can help you do this.

Coaching by Managers

Every manager is responsible for developing employees who report to them. Some managers request that their employees use this book to perform a self-assessment, and use the findings as the basis for their coaching conversations and leadership development plans. For coaching to succeed, there needs to be an understanding of the development gap. This book will help in identifying and bridging the gap for you and for others.

The Map to Leadership Mastery

THE LEADERSHIP MASTERY MAP® PROVIDES AN integrative way of thinking about leadership. We are using it as a framework to discuss all aspects of leadership.

The Leadership Mastery Map®

	Interior Subjective	Exterior Objective
Individual	VALUES BELIEFS TRAITS EMOTIONS	PHYSIOLOGY BEHAVIOR ACTIONS EXECUTION
Collective	CULTURE VALUES BELIEFS STORIES	PHYSICAL WORLD BUSINESS SCIENCE SYSTEMS

The Leadership Mastery Map® is a tool to help you see the big, or integral, picture. Two dichotomies emerge from this model: individual versus collective and subjective versus objective. With this we can see all perspectives of a particular situation.

The **upper left** quadrant of the map refers to the subjective part of you. It is the part that cannot be seen on any medical scan. This quadrant includes your values, beliefs, emotions and personality dynamics.

The **upper right** quadrant is the objective part of you as an individual. It includes your physical body and what others can objectively see about you. It also includes your behavior and your physical presence.

The **lower left** quadrant relates to the collective world. It includes those subjective dynamics that we share with others, such as the cultural values and beliefs to which our group ascribes. These groups may include our country, ethnicity, family, and the organizations with which we are affiliated.

The **lower right** quadrant, the exterior objective, is everything external to us. It includes arenas of the physical world such as the sciences, mathematics, economics and the business of doing business, including business systems.

At any particular moment, all of these quadrants are at play and inter-relating to each other. Our values and our personality influence our behavior. Our behavior influences the culture. The culture impacts how the group behaves and thus affects the performance of the organization.

Everything you do as a leader impacts all of the quadrants whether you are aware of it or not. We are therefore using this model as an integrative way of thinking about business, and as a guide in categorizing the multitude of leadership skills required in an exceptional leader.

For the purpose of this book, the subjects in the cultural quadrant also include those particularly significant leadership behaviors which impact the culture.

As you look at each quadrant, think about the degree to which you focus on each. Rate yourself on a scale of 1–5 as to the amount of time you spend on each. There is no right answer here; we are just trying to create awareness.

My inner world—my values, beliefs and personality

1   2   3   4   5

The culture of the organization

1   2   3   4   5

Execution and my behavior

1   2   3   4   5

The business of business

1   2   3   4   5

YOUR INNER WORLD

VALUES
BELIEFS
TRAITS
EMOTIONS

EXCEPTIONAL LEADERS ...
Pay Attention to Their Inner World

EXCEPTIONAL LEADERS SEE all aspects of a situation. The big picture includes inner values, beliefs, and internal dynamics. In the Leadership Mastery Map®, the upper left (individual interior subjective) should always be taken into consideration.

Our personality, character traits, values and beliefs dramatically influence how we behave as a leader. These drive our behavior. This is the reason why self-understanding is so important for effective leadership. Understanding all of these dimensions is critical.

In the news, we see many examples of individuals who have ignored their real values. Only when they find themselves negotiating a plea bargain do they realize that something went very wrong. This blindness to our values happens in less dramatic circumstances as well. We don't step back and look at all aspects of a situation, including our internal beliefs, values, and personality, before making a decision.

Perhaps we take a job or join an organization for which we are not suited. We compromise our values and beliefs, succumbing to the pressure to achieve or meet the demands of others. This, of course, can lead to considerable stress.

Many of our coaching conversations focus on the subjective internal quadrant and how it impacts the other quadrants. Without a full understanding of the inner dimensions of their being, leaders can be on automatic pilot and operate in ways that are not appropriate to a culture or the business. With greater self-awareness, there is room for more flexibility. There is room for personal growth.

 THOUGHT-PROVOKER

- Do you have a deep and clear understanding of your values?
- What are your beliefs, and how do they reveal themselves in your actions or communications?
- Are you aware of how your moods affect your behavior?
- Do you understand enough about your personality and your subsurface motivations to be able to modify your behavior for a given situation?
- Do you understand your personal worldview and are you aware of how it may differ from others?

Exceptional leaders are both self-aware and self-reflective. They are conscious about why they do what they do.

Importance (1–5)   ＿＿＿

Next Actions

EXCEPTIONAL LEADERS ...
Are Aware of Their Strengths and Limitations

EXCEPTIONAL LEADERS ARE able to assess themselves accurately. They are not in denial about either their strengths or their limitations.

Some leaders let their successes blind them to areas that they need to develop. They define themselves by material success and status and see no need to change. They suffer from "importantitis" and become narcissistic. They don't see their limitations and are not aware of their need to be on a developmental path.

To continue to be successful, leaders must be open to feedback and ensure that they have accurate information about themselves and their leadership effectiveness.

It is important for leaders to observe themselves, and to see themselves as others see them. These essential skills allow them to make adjustments in their style when necessary. Leaders should be willing to engage in self-assessment, either through formal testing and reading, or through deep personal reflection.

Armed with information about their strengths and weaknesses, leaders hire people who complement and strengthen their leadership competencies.

They also work on improving the way they lead, recognizing that there is always room for improvement regardless of how successful one is in a particular job or role.

 THOUGHT-PROVOKER

- How do you know how you come across in particularly important situations?
- Are you able to self-observe?
- Have you ever asked a confidant to give you informal feedback about how you performed in a meeting?
- Have you set up feedback systems, such as a 360-degree process, to gather feedback from others?
- Are you open to learning something new about yourself and how you lead?
- Do you have a plan in place for your own self-development?

Exceptional leaders know themselves. They capitalize on their strengths, and are continually learning. They also recognize those areas that are not their strengths and build organizational support in areas that pose a challenge for them.

Importance (1–5)   _____

Next Actions

EXCEPTIONAL LEADERS ...
Are Resilient

EXCEPTIONAL LEADERS DON'T let previous negative outcomes, upsets, and setbacks impact their effectiveness in the present. They are resilient and press on to be successful regardless of the past.

The Olympic Games offer sublime examples of resilient behavior. At the 2004 Summer Games, gymnast Paul Hamm stumbled and fell on the vault, yet minutes later performed so outstandingly in three events that he overcame his earlier low score to capture the gold medal. His mental toughness and confidence in his ability carried him beyond his previous setback, and he won the gold.

Conversely, in the tennis finals, Mardy Fish let an unfavorable umpire call upset him so much that it affected his game: he lost the gold medal to Nicholas Massou.

All leaders have business, professional, and personal setbacks in their lives. Setbacks are a part of life. Exceptional leaders are able to overcome these past upsets and perform effectively in the present. Being resilient, they focus on what can be done now and in the future.

22   The Leadership Mastery Map

 THOUGHT–PROVOKER

- How have you handled upsets and setbacks in the past?
- What have you learned from them?
- Do you avoid letting past negative outcomes affect your self-confidence?
- What ways have you learned to "shake it off" and focus on your success?
- Can you stay in the present and perform well despite setbacks?

Exceptional leaders don't let things get them down—at least not for long.

Importance (1–5) _____

Next Actions

EXCEPTIONAL LEADERS ...
Are Self-Confident

BECAUSE LEADERS KNOW their abilities, they can play to their strengths. They have an inner rudder and know that the course they choose and the action they take will be successful.

They are optimistic about taking on tough assignments and making the necessary decisions and actions to be successful.

This does not mean that leaders don't have doubts and concerns about their performance and the future. It does mean that they don't let fear drive them. They have learned to overcome fears through preparation and courage. They take bold action and inspire others to do the same.

Not only are they self-confident, their self-confidence is also apparent to others. And, this can certainly be inspiring.

Self-confidence does not mean having answers; it is a way of being that takes in all available information so a leader can make good decisions, motivate employees and move the organization forward.

Sometimes self-confidence can lead to over-insistence in the rightness of one's views to the point of discounting other points of view. True self-confidence includes a willingness to take others' points of view into consideration.

THOUGHT-PROVOKER

- How self-confident are you? Some leaders have it naturally. Others need preparation, planning, and self-reflection to gain the confidence to act.
- Think about how you come across to others. Do you convey self-confidence by communicating convincingly and directly with others?
- Do others see you as a quiet and calming presence in the organization?
- Where are you not demonstrating self-confidence? Is it with your boss? Perhaps a more experienced subordinate? Perhaps in certain group situations?
- Do you know how to practice and prepare for tough challenges so that you are self-confident?

Importance (1–5) _____

Next Actions

EXCEPTIONAL LEADERS ...
Do What's Right

EXCEPTIONAL LEADERS STAY in touch with their foundational values and focus on doing what is right.

The executives from Enron and others executives caught up in scandal, such as Martha Stewart, don't perceive themselves as crooks. However, they all found themselves sitting in prison. Something went terribly wrong.

We suspect that two significant factors were at play: one was the desire to beat the system and the other was the expectation that with a small amount of effort there would be a huge gain. If you find yourself prideful in these two areas, watch out!

One could get caught up in a culture that provides large personal payoffs but does not support one's foundational values. It takes a deep self-understanding to avoid the pressures of an organizational culture that may cause an encroachment on those values.

Without a community that reminds us what values are really important, we can go astray while deceiving ourselves that we have integrity.

Exceptional leaders are aware of these negative possibilities and keep their inner rudder straight.

THOUGHT-PROVOKER

- Do you get caught up in thinking how clever you are in being able to beat the system?
- If the payback is far greater than the effort you make, you may want to ask yourself whether you are doing the right thing.
- What beliefs are sacrosanct to you?
- What specifically do you value in life?
- Do you have a community that will remind you what is really important?

Exceptional leaders consistently practice their values and do what is right for themselves and others. They stick to their guns and set boundaries.

Importance (1–5) _____

Next Actions

EXCEPTIONAL LEADERS ...
Know Their Moods

MOODS ARE CONTAGIOUS. Leaders are designers of the moods of their organization, and exceptional leaders are aware of this. Employees are finely tuned to the mood of a leader. If the leader is in a negative mood, the mood will spread. If they are in a positive mood, that too will spread.

You can tell whether the mood in a company is upbeat, subdued, or downright depressing just by walking through employee areas.

The mood of an organization is a decisive factor in determining what the company can accomplish. Employees' moods influence how well they produce and how they relate to customers. The mood of the leader dramatically influences the mood of employees.

Sports coaches know the value of a team's mood and how it influences success. They know that a "pumped up" team generally performs better. Watch any sport and you will see examples of how a coach focuses his team's mood.

Exceptional leaders must not only know their moods, they must also be able to shift their mood positively as needed. In this way they can positively impact the employee environment.

THOUGHT-PROVOKER

- What mood are you in right now?
- Do you have your mood or does your mood have you?
- Do you smile a lot?
- Can you lighten up when called for?
- What mood are you in when you get to work in the morning?
- What is the prevalent mood of your employees who are in front of the customers and the general public?
- What strategies do you have to shift negative moods?

Almost a century ago, Dale Carnegie said, "Act enthusiastic and you will be enthusiastic!"—and so will your people.

Importance (1–5) _____

Next Actions

EXCEPTIONAL LEADERS ...
Listen to Their Gut

LISTENING TO YOUR GUT or intuition is not taught in business schools or in the office. However, most seasoned managers put it to use.

Exceptional leaders know that checking with their gut before making a decision is useful, despite the logic that says "go" or "no go."

Some leaders need dwell time to make decisions. They need to sleep on it. This allows their intuition to kick in and for them to have confidence that they are making the right decision.

Often we think of intuition as a sense or an idea that came from out of the blue. Intuition is, in fact, the result of the brain efficiently processing information, patterns, and ideas.

By developing your intuition, you can learn from experience and make confident decisions, improving your overall effectiveness as a leader.

THOUGHT-PROVOKER

- How attuned are you to your body? Do you pay attention to nagging little feelings?
- Is there a connection between your thoughts and your body? Do you ever deny your body when it is trying to tell you something?
- Have you ever said "I knew that"? Did you honor the "knowing" when it arose?
- What is the advantage of listening to and acting on your gut or intuition?
- Have there been times when you have not listened to your gut and regretted it?
- Do you take the time listen to your gut or your intuition?

Exceptional leaders know that living without utilizing their intuition or gut is like only using half a deck of cards and expecting to win the game. Use all of your natural resources—it's simply good business.

Importance (1–5) ____

Next Actions

EXCEPTIONAL LEADERS ...
Love What They Do

EXCEPTIONAL LEADERS THRIVE on being in charge and in knowing where they are going. Leaders have a good time getting there. Their excitement energizes those around them.

If you do not enjoy your job, what are the chances that you are good at it?

If there are parts of the work that you are tolerating, seek ways to change things. You might delegate to others who are more able and interested in doing it.

All of us realize we rarely enjoy every aspect of our job. Sometimes it is necessary to endure negative stuff such as excessive travel or making tough decisions which impact others.

However, when we get to the point when most of our work causes us to be unhappy, regardless of the reason, then we need to take action.

If your work is not satisfying, then do something else. Life is too short to do otherwise.

THOUGHT-PROVOKER

- How often do you say, "Boy, I love this? This is why I do what I do"?
- What percentage of the time do you say, "It's okay; I can tolerate it. This is what I do for a living"?
- What percentage of the time do you say "I hate this part? I wish I could get rid of this"?
- How often do you say, "I love working with these people"?
- How often do you say, "I can tolerate working with these people, just as long as I don't have to deal with them too much"?
- How often do you say, "I can't stand working with these people"?

Exceptional leaders know that loving what you do makes life worthwhile.

Importance (1–5) _____

Next Actions

EXCEPTIONAL LEADERS ...
Think Strategically

IT TAKES MORE THAN operational effectiveness to succeed in a changing business environment. Exceptional Leaders think strategically. There are two aspects of strategic thinking: seeing the whole picture, and seeing where you want to go in the future.

Leaders see the whole picture. Their thinking needs to be broad, taking more than just their areas of day-to-day focus into consideration. Leaders realize that all aspects of the business are interdependent and interconnected. The Leadership Mastery Map provides the opportunity to see all facets of a landscape strategically.

Leaders also need to identify the future they wish to create. They need to look at the current situation holistically and determine the desired future. Once there is clarity they can declare the desired future and get everyone aligned to create it.

Some leaders are naturally future-oriented. Others tend to focus on current operational imperatives. There needs to be a balance between the two in order to run an organization successfully.

THOUGHT-PROVOKER

- Are you stuck in the weeds of day-to-day demands?
- Does your schedule allow you time to step back, think, and plan? A plan is not a plan unless it is put in writing.
- What future would you like to create for your organization?
- Do you begin with the end in mind, articulating for yourself and others the future you want to achieve?
- Do you bring others into collaboration to benefit from different ways of thinking?

Exceptional leaders not only see the trees *and* the forest but also the horizon and what's over the next hill. Then they lead to achieve their vision.

Importance (1–5)   _____

Next Actions

NOTES

YOUR ACTIONS

PHYSIOLOGY
BEHAVIOR
ACTIONS
EXECUTION

EXCEPTIONAL LEADERS ...
Plan and Take Appropriate Action

IN THE LEADERSHIP MASTERY MAP, the upper right quadrant (the exterior individual objective) consists of one's physical body and one's behavior. It is the objective behavior that others can see.

Exceptional leaders take appropriate action in light of all the other quadrants, i.e. their individual internal dynamics such as personality and values from the upper left quadrant; the collective internal dynamics such as culture from the lower left quadrant; and the external objective dynamics such as the commercial business logic and objectives in a particular situation from the lower right quadrant. They set goals for themselves and achieve measurable outcomes. They are able to execute tasks and lead others to execute them as well.

The upper right quadrant also deals with your physical body. Health issues may arise when all quadrants are not congruent—for instance, when one's actions (upper right quadrant) are not compatible with one's values (upper left quadrant), or when one's personality (upper left quadrant) is not suited to the requirements of the job (lower right quadrant).

THOUGHT–PROVOKER

- Do you have clearly defined goals?
- Do you clearly or consistently take the necessary actions to achieve your goals?
- Do you have a system to measure the impact of your actions on a particular situation as well as on other people?
- Are you physically capable of taking the action needed in a particular situation?
- Do you pay attention to your body and your well-being?
- Do you pay attention to your staff's physical well-being?

Exceptional leaders are able to execute plans consistently with high quality.

Importance (1–5)   ____

Next Actions

EXCEPTIONAL LEADERS ...
Admit When They Are Wrong

None of us are perfect and yet some leaders act as if they are. They don't seem capable of admitting when they have made a mistake or a bad decision. Fear may drive their need to look good and to be perceived as a perfect leader.

One of Dale Carnegie's principles in his book *How to Win Friends and Influence People* is that when one is wrong, admit it quickly and emphatically.

When a leader ricochets blame to others or simply lets others take the blame, it negatively impacts their credibility and the trust of others.

Not admitting to a mistake points to an unwillingness to learn and sets up a culture where employees do only what they are asked to do and mistakes are covered up.

Being willing to admit mistakes creates an open culture that encourages risk-taking and honesty where employees can learn and grow and the organization can prosper.

Exceptional Leaders are willing to take responsibility for mistakes and encourage others to do the same.

THOUGHT-PROVOKER

- When was the last time you admitted a mistake?
- When you have admitted a mistake, what has been the impact on those around you?
- Do you have a culture where others are comfortable in making decisions, taking risks and truly leading the organization forward?

Exceptional leaders know that by owning errors they actually build credibility and trust and create a healthy culture that fosters openness and risk-taking.

Importance (1–5)   ____

Next Actions

EXCEPTIONAL LEADERS ...
Align Their Body with Their Intentions

THE WAY YOU CARRY yourself has an impact on how others perceive you. Your bearing should convey confidence, poise, decisiveness, and openness. However, it may convey arrogance, aloofness, indecisiveness, and powerlessness.

Your posture can also have a significant effect on your internal state. Are you ambitious and full of energy, or are you listless and resigned?

How you carry your body influences your mood and what you can achieve. Concave chest, stooped shoulders, slow movements, and shallow breathing lead to disempowered states, while erectness, deep breathing, and sureness of movement can be empowering.

One of our clients held his body and walked in a manner that others perceived as not powerful. We suggested that he walk faster and more confidently, that he take up more of the hallway. He reported that the impression he made on others changed dramatically once he made these adjustments in how he moved through the world.

When you adjust your physical bearing, new behaviors become possible.

THOUGHT-PROVOKER

- Do you stand tall?
- Do you move through the world with confidence?
- What does your posture convey to others?
- When you observe others, do you make judgments based on how they hold their body? Does it make sense that others do so with you?
- Have you tried to shift your mood by changing your posture, your pace, or how you sit in meetings?

Exceptional leaders know that their posture is a factor in how they influence others as well as determining their internal state such as their moods and behaviors.

Importance (1–5) ____

Next Actions

EXCEPTIONAL LEADERS ...
Are Demanding

EXCEPTIONAL LEADERS CHALLENGE and stretch their people all the time.

Being demanding does not require being autocratic. Rather, it means communicating your expectations of superior work, and giving constructive feedback to those who do not meet these expectations. This is a common approach used by exceptional sports coaches and school teachers.

Most people want to do a good job, and are naturally motivated. However, leaders need to create an environment where others can excel. They need to communicate high expectations. Others will respond to this and want to accomplish great things.

Expectations should be more that saying "do better" or "do more". They should be specifically articulated so that others can really embrace what it takes to excel. Everyone should know the criteria for excellence so they know when they meet it.

If a leader does not communicate effectively or is satisfied with less than excellence, performance will ratchet downward toward mediocrity.

THOUGHT-PROVOKER

- How does your performance match up with your personal standards? You can't expect others to do their best if you don't do yours.
- Have you communicated your standards for excellence?
- Scan your horizon for the people who have the most influence on the success of your organization and on you. Are they performing up to your standards?
- Are they performing to a standard that will allow the organization to meet its goals?
- If not, be willing to take action. Open up the conversation about performance and communicate expectations, clearly stating the standards for excellence.

Being relaxed about your performance and the performance of others is a recipe for mediocrity.

Importance (1–5) ＿＿＿

Next Actions

EXCEPTIONAL LEADERS ...
Are Not Too Loyal

Can you be too loyal? You can, if your loyalty to one person negatively impacts your organization's effectiveness.

Loyalty may blind others to the truth about an employee's value or competency. This is particularly prevalent when family members are in the business. A long business and personal relationship with someone who becomes like family is another kind of nepotism. This can breed a tolerance for bad behavior and incompetence.

If an employee has a special relationship with someone higher up in the organization, there is a potential for political shenanigans that can be detrimental to others in the company and cause them to not take actions that should be taken.

Exceptional Leaders are alert to the impact of their special relationship to individuals in the organization and do not let this get in the way of making appropriate decisions that everyone knows should be made.

THOUGHT-PROVOKER

- As a leader, do you have any special close relationships to others in your organization?
- How do these relationships influence your making appropriate decisions regarding them?
- Do you put more credence in the messages from these folks over others: not because they have more credibility but simply that you know them better?
- Are you willing to get the entire picture and consult others to insure that you are not biased in ways that are harmful to others and the organization?

Exceptional leaders don't let their loyalty override their willingness to be objective on people decisions.

Importance (1–5)   ____

Next Actions

EXCEPTIONAL LEADERS ...
Are Not Too Busy

YOU SHOULD NOT BE too busy to get to essentials. In today's world, it is very easy to get sucked into non-essentials, such as constantly checking e-mail and voicemail, rather than attending to priorities.

Sometimes we get sucked into the fast pace of today's life and the ever-present huge amounts of information, entertainment and distractions coming at us. We lose our focus.

"Busyness" should not be used as an excuse to avoid tough decisions or unpleasant, but necessary, conversations. Nor should it be a way to avoid working on high-payoff projects.

Being busy should not be a reason for not maintaining relationships within an organization that are important to your success. Take the necessary time to converse with direct reports, peers, customers, and all other stakeholders. Conversations mean there is a relationship. No conversations mean there is no relationship.

The exceptional leader knows that focusing *only* on urgent and important issues, although critical, may not lead to long-term progress.

Leaders must also focus on important, but less urgent, matters that will yield the best long-term results. This includes high-payoff projects and cultivating important relationships.

THOUGHT-PROVOKER

- Does your busyness create denial about what is really important and essential to the success of your organization?
- Do you let others fill your calendar at the expense of having the necessary reflective and planning time that you need to be successful?
- Do you let your busyness interfere with setting up systems that increase your efficiency and allow you to focus on more important matters?
- Do you get so immersed in the day-to-day stuff that you cannot see the big picture?
- Do you get so immersed in the day-to-day stuff that you don't attend to important relationships? Who do you need to call right now?

Exceptional leaders stick to essentials and avoid busyness, which diminishes their leadership effectiveness.

Importance (1–5) _____

Next Actions

EXCEPTIONAL LEADERS ...
Are Persistent

DIFFICULT AND CHALLENGING ENDEAVORS require persistence, which is the twin sister of excellence. Excellence is a matter of quality; persistence is a matter of time.

Calvin Coolidge said,

> Nothing in this world can take the place of persistence. Talent will not; nothing is more common than unsuccessful people with talent. Genius will not; unrewarded genius is almost a proverb. Education will not; the world is full of educated derelicts. Persistence and determination alone are omnipotent. The slogan 'press on' has solved and always will solve the problems of the human race.

So when the going gets tough, exceptional leaders get going. They inspire themselves and others to persevere in the face of difficulties in order to achieve important goals and realize their vision.

THOUGHT-PROVOKER

- Are you discouraged and giving up on something in your personal or professional life because it is difficult?
- What are the potential costs of not succeeding—both to you and to your organization?
- What barriers do you need to overcome?
- What forces do you need to bear?
- Have you created, and fully communicated, such a compelling future that others are willing to persevere in order to achieve it?
- Do you inspire others in your organization to persevere?

Exceptional leaders stay the course until they succeed.

Importance (1–5)   ____

Next Actions

EXCEPTIONAL LEADERS ...
Are Personally Productive

A SURVEY OF NEW YEAR'S resolutions revealed that 59 percent of the respondents wished to improve their time management and productivity.

Leadership, a demanding endeavor, requires focused, sustained energy and personal efficiency. Exceptional leaders must be efficient and utilize their time effectively to be successful.

Efficiency can be achieved through maximizing the tools and resources at your disposal and also by improving on your personal systems and daily habits.

Technology has consistently increased our productivity. Exceptional leaders are early adopters of technology that will improve their personal effectiveness. They are not afraid of change or to learn new things.

Exceptional leaders also use others, such as administrative assistants, to leverage their efforts and to improve their overall productivity.

THOUGHT-PROVOKER

- Do you have a well-designed time management system?
- Does this system allow you to work on those important but less urgent matters that will make a difference in your long-term success?
- Do you know the full capabilities of your electronic calendar? Some leaders color code their calendars so they can see how they use their time.
- Do you reprioritize based on changing circumstances? At the same time, do you avoid being whipsawed by extraneous external demands or distractions?
- Do you delegate effectively, maximizing the capabilities of administrators and direct reports so that you can focus on high-priority, big-picture areas?
- Do unproductive meetings suck up valuable time that could be used to make a significant impact?
- Do you have dedicated time to work e-mail, or are you at the real time mercy of e-mail such that it is more of a distraction than a communication tool?

Exceptional leaders constantly look for ways to be more productive.

Importance (1–5)   ____

Next Actions

EXCEPTIONAL LEADERS ...
Are Willing to Make Tough Decisions

"IN ANY MOMENT of decision, the best thing is to do the right thing; the next best thing is to do the wrong thing; and the worst thing to do is nothing." *Theodore Roosevelt*

It can be difficult to know the right time to make a decision, but at the same time, not making a decision is a decision.

Making decisions that negatively affect others, such as discipline or termination, is rarely done with joy. However, such decisions need to be made from time to time for the sake of the organization and its success.

Reversing previous decisions can be tough. It may require admitting that the first decision was a mistake.

Sometimes the potential consequences of a decision can be huge. Consider Eisenhower deciding on the timing of the invasion of Normandy.

Executives sometimes make decisions on capital investment that are literally "bet the company" types of decisions. Boeing comes to mind when, for example, it decides on a new billion dollar commercial aircraft.

THOUGHT-PROVOKER

- Are there areas where you may be postponing a tough decision?
- Why are you waiting?
- What are the consequences of not making a decision?
- Is there a concern about timing? What conditions have to exist for you to know the time is right?
- Do you need to enlist others to get their support? What and with whom do you need to communicate?
- Does your heart tell you not to take action and your head tell you not to? Maybe your head says "no" and your gut says "go." How will you align both?

Exceptional leaders have the courage to make the decisions necessary to move their organizations forward. It is simply part of their job.

Importance (1–5)   _____

Next Actions

EXCEPTIONAL LEADERS ...
Are Willing to Take Risks

FULL MASTERY OF ANYTHING requires that one experiences both successes that reinforce and failures that deepen learning. Only then will one truly master a skill.

Leaders must be willing to make decisions. Decisions require taking risks.

Taking risks is not only important for the payoffs but also for the learning. For this reason, the exceptional leader is willing to take the risks associated with doing things that are out of their comfort zone.

Risks may be as small as trying new approaches in dealing with others, such as confronting unpleasant situations and having uncomfortable conversations. Changing one's behavior certainly can feel risky.

Other risks can be more consequential, such as making decisions where your, or another person's, job is on the line. This can involve business decisions that have political consequences. And it can also involve decisions to support one's values.

THOUGHT-PROVOKER

- What is it you are not doing for fear of failure, rejection, or loss?
- What would you do now if you moved through your fear and took action?
- What products would you produce? Would you give that speech? Would you leave that unsatisfying job, not knowing with certainty what is next?
- Would you take an assignment that would be particularly challenging with high risk but that would also come with a huge payoff? Would you start that new business, or make that investment now with an uncertain but highly profitable potential return in the future?
- Would you make those needed personnel changes?

Exceptional leaders are willing to take risks. Feel the fear, and do it anyway. Move out of your comfort zone. The exceptional leader knows that risk is an inherent part of the game.

Importance (1–5)   ____

Next Actions

EXCEPTIONAL LEADERS ...
Are Masterful Recruiters

IN TODAY'S WAR for top talent, leaders have to be masterful recruiters. The market for talent seems to be more competitive every day. Good candidates are hard to find and receive multiple offers. All of this impacts retention and the capability to achieve business results.

Recruiting requires senior executive commitment. Exceptional leaders know that they must personally focus on getting and keeping the right people to make their organization successful.

Many leaders keep their networks open and are in the business of always looking for top talent. They keep certain people in mind should a need arise.

They attend to what is going on in the recruiting effort and participate in selling the organization to prospective employees. They make sure that all the necessary resources, money and staffing are available to meet recruitment objectives.

They ensure that that their organization has a strong reputation, a good "employment brand" so that it is seen as an attractive place to work and build a career.

THOUGHT-PROVOKER

- Do you have a comprehensive talent strategy that provides flexibility to meet planned and unplanned human capital and knowledge needs?
- Are you aware of your company's employment brand?
- Do you have a systematic, leading-edge recruiting process that produces the results you need?
- Are you constantly sourcing new talent?
- Are you sufficiently flexible in your negotiations during the offer stage?
- Are your frontline managers leading in a way that will allow you to retain and recruit top people?

Exceptional leaders know that "getting the right people on the bus" is essential to success, and they make every effort to find those people. [10]

Importance (1–5) ____

Next Actions

EXCEPTIONAL LEADERS ...
Avoid Attention Overwhelm

THOSE WHO EXPERIENCE "attention overwhelm" lose focus, productivity, interpersonal effectiveness, and the ability to meet top priorities.

All of us see that the sheer information coming at us is growing exponentially. The deluge of input and analysis required in today's business environment can overload the brain. When you are faced with the 110th e-mail and demands for three decisions without enough information in the midst of the fifth interruption while preparing for an international trip and/or a board meeting, attention overwhelm is almost certain.

Exceptional leaders know that they must set boundaries and aggressively manage their environments rather than work at the mercy of their environments.

Setting boundaries means being willing to say no. Saying no, even to your boss if necessary, means that you can focus on high-payoff activities and not be at the mercy of trivia or low priority items.

Managing your environment means shutting down certain non-essential activities and sources of distraction in order to concentrate.

THOUGHT-PROVOKER

- Do you know when you are overwhelmed and why?
- Do you experience stress due to being overwhelmed?
- Do you manage your e-mail, or does it manage you?
- Do you control your calendar, or do others?
- Do you take the time to regroup and just think?
- Are there things that you can simply stop attending to that will free up your time and space?
- Do you set boundaries with your colleagues to ensure that you focus on what is really important to your success?
- Do you take enough time off?

Exceptional leaders manage their environments so they don't become overwhelmed.

Importance (1–5)   ____

Next Actions

EXCEPTIONAL LEADERS ...
Balance Advocacy and Inquiry

LEADERS ARE USUALLY IN ONE OF TWO MODES: advocating or inquiring. Most leaders default to advocating or, in other words, selling. They believe they know the shortest and right route to achieve their goals and they are going to sell others on moving ahead. As a result, many conversations are reduced to a "yes, but" mode where there is no real listening. The leader does not suspend judgment to make room for fully inquiring into others' points of view.

It takes effort to shift one's level of consciousness out of an advocacy mode, and to be truly curious; to deepen understanding. The payback can be extraordinary, not only in getting buy-in but, most importantly, improving results by getting other ideas and approaches. Once employees feel that they have been heard, they can be inspired.

Some leaders default to inquiry and are not good advocates. They don't sell their ideas when needed. They don't inspire others to achieve. They need to be able to sell in order to energize others.

Exceptional leaders can easily shift into one mode or the other depending on the situation.

THOUGHT-PROVOKER

- Which is your default: advocacy or inquiry?
- In conversations, do you respond immediately, restating your views, rather than asking clarifying questions to fully explore other points of view?
- What would be the benefit of your being able to easily shift from advocacy to inquiry or vice versa?
- How would your colleagues respond to you being in an inquiring mode more often?
- Do you get other perspectives first, before pushing your ideas as the right ones?
- Are you able to push your ideas ahead after fully exploring other points of view?

Exceptional leaders are flexible. They can balance inquiring and advocating while getting outstanding results.

Importance (1–5)   ____

Next Actions

EXCEPTIONAL LEADERS ...
Challenge the Status Quo

IF YOU DON'T CHALLENGE the status quo, the external world will. With today's level of accelerating change, organizations and their leaders must respond appropriately to changing conditions in the market, in their industries, and in their organizations' cultures.

Technology has transformed our business and personal lives: and it will continue to be a disruptive influence on our business, requiring leaders to be responsive and agile. Standing still is not an option.

Leaders must constantly scan their organizations and their management teams to find opportunities for change that will meet external demands. They must avoid getting stuck in the status quo through the natural inertia we all succumb to from time to time.

Faced with a "this is the way we have always done it" mentality, it is necessary for the leader to encourage others to be willing to change and to look at things in light of current circumstances and future needs.

THOUGHT-PROVOKER

- Look for people and systems that have been doing things the same way for three years or more. Challenge whether it remains the best way. Where could it be improved?
- Do you have a systematic way of keeping up with current industry trends?
- Can your competition make a significant change that will impact your business?
- Do you anticipate upcoming changes in the culture and how they will impact your organization? The pending retirement of the Boomers and the emergence of Generation Y (born 1980–2000) are examples.
- Do your technical systems allow you to maintain your competitive edge?
- Do you know where you are on the product life cycle and how to keep up?

Remember, if you don't change and grow, you die.

Importance (1–5) ____

Next Actions

EXCEPTIONAL LEADERS ...
Declare the Future

OUR FOUNDING FATHERS declared our independence. To create a desired future, a leader must declare it. The declaration then creates the space, energy, and enthusiasm for the leader and others to make it a reality.

Bill Gates' declaration called for "a computer on every desk running Microsoft software." This has been realized, and Microsoft is struggling to find the next declaration to propel the company into the future.

Google's mission is "to organize the world's information and make it universally accessible and useful." This declaration certainly seems to be working for Google.

A few decades ago, Jimmy Carter declared that our country suffered from malaise and got into big trouble for it. Reagan came along, made positive declarations about America's future, and was elected.

Declarations, even with a short-term perspective, can be powerful. Examples are "We will increase sales by 20 percent next year," and "We will launch this product by March 1st."

If you want motivate your employees, declare a compelling future for them and for your organization.

THOUGHT-PROVOKER

- What future have you declared for yourself?
- What future have you declared for your organization?
- As a leader, do you inspire others by declaring the future?
- Have you made your declarations public?
- Have you made them in writing?
- Have you made speeches declaring to all stakeholders what you want to create for your organization?

Exceptional leaders declare the future powerfully and frequently to all who will listen.

Importance (1–5)   ____

Next Actions

EXCEPTIONAL LEADERS ...
Don't Hunker Down

WHEN TIMES ARE TOUGH, there is a temptation to hide out in order to avoid the shame of things not going well. Ego can be tied to one's job responsibility and most of us don't do shame well. Hiding might mean focusing on just the numbers and internal dynamics that must be managed during financial difficulties. One's head is down and concentrating with a short term focus.

Exceptional leaders know that they must expand their horizon and engage all stakeholders in tough times. Connecting stakeholders to the longer term vision of new possibilities inspires them to support tough decisions and critical goals.

This means having constructive conversations with vendors when payables are extended; keeping employees abreast of the truth of the situation; managing relationships with customers and attaining new customers, as well as regularly communicating and negotiating with bankers and equity shareholders.

When this is done and everyone is aware of the realities and initiatives being taken, exceptional leaders will have the greatest chance of prevailing during difficult times.

THOUGHT-PROVOKER

- In what ways might you be hunkered down?
- Have you cut back on marketing rather than looking at the longer term?
- Are vendors and suppliers fully apprised of your situation so that accommodations might be negotiated?
- Are employees inspired to stay the course?
- Are you out and about or are you in your office a lot?
- Are your bankers being kept fully up to date so that they can help?
- Do the board and shareholders know what is going on and what your plans are to address challenges?

Exceptional leaders don't hunker down in tough times. They are present and accessible.

Importance (1–5)   ____

Next Actions

EXCEPTIONAL LEADERS ...
Don't Rest on Their Laurels

IN TODAY'S FAST-PACED BUSINESS world, the expression "What have you done for me lately?" is even more of an imperative. Leaders have high expectations of their employees, and organizations have high expectations of their leaders.

Some employees take such pride their accomplishments that they don't realize that they need to continually add value.

It is fine to take pride in accomplishments. But previous accomplishments are not a reason for current entitlement. Leaders must produce in the present and focus on the future, rather than on past glories.

Even in retirement, high profile executives, such as Lee Iacocca and Jack Welsh, remain in the game by writing best-selling books and consulting rather than focusing on the past.

THOUGHT-PROVOKER

- To what degree do you focus on past glories?
- Does anyone in your organization "rest on his laurels"?
- Do current stakeholders, including your boss, really care about what you accomplished five, ten, or twenty years ago?
- Do you keep up with current trends, new technology, and ways of thinking?
- Do you criticize others because something they do is not the way something was done in the past?
- What adjustments do you need to make to continue to be a highly valued asset to your organization?

Exceptional leaders take satisfaction from their accomplishments and keep in the game of value creation for the present and the future.

Importance (1–5)   ____

Next Actions

EXCEPTIONAL LEADERS ...
Don't Try To Be Heroes

HEROES ARE LONERS. They see what needs to be done, they know the right way to do it, and they swoop in and save the day. Heroes of myth and in the news are the ones who rescue. They generally work, not in a team, but by themselves. They are so competent, capable, and astute that they don't need any help.

Exceptional leaders know that they must truly partner with others to make their organization successful. If they take a heroic attitude, they may lose the brilliance and perspective that others can bring. Expecting others to check their brain at the door because you are the only one that is capable and knows what needs to be done is not the best way to capitalize on what others can contribute.

Lebron James, one of the top NBA basketball players, says that his primary focus is not on his performance, but on supporting his team to excel. He recognizes the gifts that his team brings to his success. He knows it is not all about him.

Exceptional leaders are more ambitious for the team and the organization than themselves.

THOUGHT-PROVOKER

- Do you have a heroic mentality?
- Are you the appointed one (by others or yourself) to save the day?
- How does a heroic attitude influence the way you work with others and build teams?
- What attitudes are generated in others if you are the only one with the right answers and the right way to do things?
- Can you observe yourself when you get into a heroic attitude?

Exceptional leaders know that it is not all about them. They team with others and extract their ideas, expertise and insights to achieve organizational goals.

Importance (1–5)   ____

Next Actions

EXCEPTIONAL LEADERS ...
Exhibit Self-Control

LEADERS WITH EMOTIONAL self-control are able to manage disturbing emotions and impulses, and even channel these feelings in useful ways. Exceptional leaders stay calm and clear-headed under stress or during a crisis. [11]

Some leaders exhibit highly stressful, unproductive behavior and are unable to contain themselves—acting out like a two-year-old with tantrums. This behavior is disrespectful of other people's dignity, and can have devastating effects on everyone involved.

Other leaders exhibit stress behavior through impatience and irritability, interrupting others, not listening, putting others down, and discounting their ideas.

It is fine to be passionate and impatient for results. Effective leadership is demanding. Anger and frustration are okay at times, provided they are held in check and result in productive behavior.

This is a graphic example of how a leader's behavior which is in the upper right quadrant may have significant influence on the culture of an organization, which is in the lower left quadrant. A leader can leave a negative emotional wake impacting the morale, attitudes and emotions of those with whom they interface.

THOUGHT-PROVOKER

- To what degree are you aware of your emotions?
- Do you display anger appropriately?
- Do you know what triggers your stress reactions?
- Can you observe yourself and see how your behavior impacts others?
- Are you able to catch yourself when internal pressure builds, and shift your emotions so that your behavior remains productive?
- Do you have confidants who can observe you and give you feedback when they see things getting out of hand?

Exceptional leaders are able to control their impulses under stress and behave in productive and effective ways rather than destructive ways.

Importance (1–5) ____

Next Actions

EXCEPTIONAL LEADERS ...
Focus

EXCEPTIONAL LEADERS prioritize and focus on the truly important.

In an extensive interview with Warren Buffett, TV personality Charlie Rose asked him the secret to his phenomenal success as a businessman, through which he has become the second richest man in the world. Buffett's simple answer was his ability to focus. He picks just the right thing to concentrate on.

He does extensive research and finds companies that meet specific criteria for him to invest in. Those criteria include employing the right people. Then he lets them run the companies and stays for the long haul. That's it. It helps, of course, that he happens to be brilliant.

Exceptional leaders find high-payoff activities to engage in and think about. They focus. They decide and take action.

THOUGHT-PROVOKER

- Do you really know what business you are in?
- Can you turn down business because it is not suitable?
- Do you know where you need to focus your attention and your actions to ensure the biggest payoff for your business?
- How much time do you waste on unimportant, low-priority, low-payoff activities?
- Have you set up systems and routines so you avoid being drained or scattered by extraneous and low-payoff activities?
- Have you set boundaries to ensure that others respect your priorities?

Exceptional leaders constantly assess where they can best use their time and attention. They simply and powerfully focus.

Importance (1–5)   _____

Next Actions

EXCEPTIONAL LEADERS ...
Have Bandwidth

ONE OF THE ISSUES that Microsoft has is that its employees can't get onto their leaders' calendars. The leaders are spread so thin with bureaucratic activities that they can't attend to employees' creativity or their needs for decisions.

Some say that this lack of executive bandwidth has slowed the organization down, allowing Google and Apple to beat them out in the search engine, digital music, and cell phone businesses.

Exceptional leaders create the necessary time bandwidth for them to manage their employees effectively. They do not become a bottle neck for decisions. This may mean reducing the number of direct reports or redesigning how they work. It may mean relentlessly prioritizing and reprioritizing so they are available to ensure that their employees get the face time needed to move initiatives forward.

THOUGHT-PROVOKER

- Are you too busy to see everyone who needs your support?
- Can the right people get onto your calendar easily? Are the wrong people getting onto it too easily and taking your time with unimportant things?
- Does your calendar reflect your priorities? Are you engaged in short-term-focused endeavors or in long-term, bigger payoff endeavors?
- Do you attend unimportant meetings?
- Do you make time to inspire others to focus creatively on the future?

A leader's time is extremely valuable. Exceptional leaders use their time wisely.

Importance (1–5)   ____

Next Actions

EXCEPTIONAL LEADERS ...
Keep Their Promises

EXCEPTIONAL LEADERS know that keeping promises is essential for themselves and their organization to build and maintain trust.

Leadership requires making effective requests. When you agree to a request, it becomes a promise. For trust to exist, promises must be kept.

Execution demands accountability. Accountability involves keeping promises.

Exceptional leaders keep their promises on little things, such as being on time to meetings, as well as big things. They know that they set the tone for the entire organization. If they don't keep their promises to customers, to employees, and to all other stakeholders, they will be giving tacit permission for others to do the same.

THOUGHT-PROVOKER

- Do you know when you have made a promise?
- Do you communicate your promises clearly so there is no misunderstanding?
- Are your promises slippery (e.g., "I will try to do it")?
- Have you made any promises that you have not fulfilled?
- Do you show up for meetings on time?
- Have you made requests that have not been acted upon or followed up on?
- Have you established a culture of commitment within your organization that supports keeping promises and holding others accountable?

Exceptional leaders make effective make requests and keep promises knowing it is essential for organizational success.

Importance (1–5)   ____

Next Actions

EXCEPTIONAL LEADERS ...
Keep Things on Course

EXCEPTIONAL LEADERS CHART the course to a successful future. They make sure that things go according to plan and make mid-course corrections when and where needed. Assuming that everything is going okay can lead to lots of trouble.

Exceptional leaders set up systems to ensure that they are kept in the loop as things progress. This could include reports from others in writing, personally, or in meetings. It could include "management by walking around" to see how things are going.

Leaders set up communication loops so they are notified immediately when plans are off track. They ask questions. They hold others accountable. They reinforce expectations where needed. They bring in additional resources. They rethink things and take new approaches.

They demonstrate a commitment to being successful.

THOUGHT-PROVOKER

- Have you declared a future for yourself and others?
- Do you have a system to ensure that things go according to plan?
- Do you direct and redirect others when things break down and do not proceed as you expect?
- Do you take responsibility for the success of an endeavor and yet hold others accountable for execution?
- Do you get things back on track?

Exceptional leaders are aware of how things are going and take appropriate action when and where needed to ensure success.

Importance (1–5)   ____

Next Actions

EXCEPTIONAL LEADERS ...
Know What Kind of Power to Use

POWER IS THE CAPABILITY to get others to do things. Exceptional leaders recognize several types of power that they can use, depending on the circumstances. In today's complex flat and matrix organizations, traditional hierarchical power may not be sufficient to succeed.

Hierarchical power is a top-down form of power based on the ability to reward and punish.

Referent Power is the power derived from the relationship with someone with hierarchical power, such as the boss.

Personal power is the power of one's personality, exerted through communication and persuasion.

Charismatic power comes from being an attractive and natural leader others simply want to follow.

Expert power comes from one's expertise—having solutions and knowing what needs to be done.

Collaborative power relies on relationship skills, as well as the willingness and ability to add value to the efforts of others.

Relationship power comes by knowing the right people and influencing them to assist your agenda.

Emotional power is the ability to impact the moods and emotions of those around you.

 THOUGHT-PROVOKER

- What type of power do you use as a leader?
- What combinations of the types of power do you use?
- Which type of power can you add to increase your effectiveness?
- If you are not competent in the use of a particular type of power, do you have a path for improvement?

Exceptional leaders use several types of power concurrently, depending on what is needed, to lead an organization to success.

Importance (1–5) _____

Next Actions

EXCEPTIONAL LEADERS ...
Lead Masterfully During a Crisis

TERRORIST ATTACKS AND WEATHER DISASTERS, cause us to reflect on the leadership characteristics needed in a time of crisis.

Leading during a crisis requires a special understanding of how people react to loss and what they need from a leader to get through their personal challenges.

First, leaders need to empathize and communicate their understanding. They don't sugarcoat the facts, eroding credibility. Leaders must encourage others to face the brutal reality of a situation. This helps others to move through shock and disbelief. Leaders do this by communicating empathetically, often and repeatedly.

Leaders need to inspire others to believe that they will ultimately prevail and overcome whatever difficulties they face. They must inspire others to have confidence in themselves.

Admiral Stockdale displayed this type of leadership in the Hanoi Hilton, inspiring others to face the reality of the situation while having unswerving faith that they would eventually prevail.[2]

Winston Churchill displayed that kind of leadership during the London Blitz, as did Mayor Rudy Giuliani after the 9/11 attack.

Leaders should reassure others that action is being taken. They need to tell the truth. Simply saying what others want to hear erodes credibility, if a leader's words are not backed up by facts and action.

Those touched by a crisis feel many emotions, such as fear, anger, resentment, and anxiety about the future. Complaints and concerns will be expressed. Leaders listen and take action to address concerns.

 THOUGHT-PROVOKER

- Can you honestly listen and empathize with those in a crisis?
- Do you tend to sugarcoat bad news, telling others what you think they want to hear? Or do you help others face the reality of a situation?
- Do you regularly communicate during periods of shock and disbelief?
- Can you inspire others to have unswerving faith that they will prevail, that they will get through the crisis?
- Do you reassure others that action is being taken and then follow up on your commitments?
- Do you tell the truth no matter how bad it is?

Exceptional leaders inspire others to rise to the occasion despite difficulties and challenges.

Importance (1–5)   _____

Next Actions

EXCEPTIONAL LEADERS ...
Make Contingency Plans

HURRICANES KATRINA AND RITA AND MOST RECENTLY SANDY have highlighted the need for leaders to make contingency plans should unlikely, negative events occur.

Exceptional leaders know that bad things happen quickly while good things generally happen slowly. While no one can predict the future, those who plan for the unexpected certainly fare better than those who don't.

Having a plan gives comfort. Having a plan avoids the panic caused by not being in control. Having a plan means recovering more quickly from an unexpected negative event.

After shutting down when the World Trade Center was attacked, Merrill Lynch moved its operations from the financial center in Manhattan to backup locations in New Jersey. Within five days, the company's technology was up and running with employees at their desks. This required extraordinary prior contingency planning.

THOUGHT-PROVOKER

- What would be on a list of possible catastrophes for your organization?
- Have you thought through the consequences of unexpected negative future events?
- Do you have written plans to account for those consequences?
- Do you have prudent insurance that you can reasonably afford? What risks are not covered?
- Do you have primary and secondary backups for all electronic information that is vital to your business operations?
- Do you have alternatives to quickly re-acquire resources that are vital to business operations?

Exceptional leaders know how to measure and manage risk, developing necessary contingency plans to deal with improbable but potential events.

Importance (1–5)   ____

Next Actions

EXCEPTIONAL LEADERS ...
Make Effective Requests

EXCEPTIONAL LEADERS use language masterfully to coordinate action. This includes making effective requests.

When making a request, they communicate the conditions of satisfaction they expect and when they want the requested action taken. Most importantly, the request is clearly communicated

---

THOUGHT-PROVOKER

When you make requests, use the following to ensure you that you get what you want with the quality you expect, when you want it.

CAN DO

Is the person you are making the request of personally capable of doing what is requested? Are they competent to do it?

Does the system allow them to do it?

Do they have the resources to do it?

Does the requested time frame recognize their priorities?

Will they be able to meet the conditions of satisfaction associated with the request?

WANT TO

Are they generally a motivated person?

Do they know the reason for the request?

Is it within the scope of their responsibilities?

WILL DO

Does the person you are making the request of agree to the request? In other words, will they promise to do it?

Do they have the power to say no or to negotiate the conditions of the request?

DO

Do they honor their commitment or communicate the reason why they can't in a timely manner?

Requests and promises make the world go round. An exceptional leader must make them effectively.

Importance (1–5)   ____

Next Actions

EXCEPTIONAL LEADERS ...
Make Good Decisions

   "A DECISION IS A JUDGMENT. It is a choice between alternatives. It is rarely a choice between right and wrong. It is at best a choice between almost right and probably wrong—but much more often a choice between two courses of action, neither of which is probably more nearly right than the other." Peter Drucker[3]

Do you have a process for decision-making? The "Thought-Provoker" below describes one process to ensure that most of your decisions are almost right.

THOUGHT-PROVOKER

What is the situation/problem?

- Determine whether to write an analysis of the problem. If the decision is important, write it out.
- What are my objectives?
- When considering each of the quadrants, what do I want to achieve in the short- and long-term?

Who and when?

Do I need to make this decision, or should someone else make it? When do I need to make this decision? Who will be touched by this decision?

What are my options?

Analyze the options. What are the positive and negative consequences of each option in terms of people (culture), time, and money (the business)? What are the short- and long-term implications of each option? Which option best meets your objectives?

How do you best communicate?

Do I need to involve others, for either their opinions or their buy-in?

Decide

After deciding and before taking action, assess whether the decision feels right. Trust your intuition.

Implement

What are the timelines and milestones? With whom do you need to communicate?

Evaluate

How will you know that you've made a good decision? Have all of your objectives been met? Do you need to make adjustments?

Importance (1–5) ____

Next Actions

EXCEPTIONAL LEADERS ...
Manage by Commitment

EXCEPTIONAL LEADERS know that agreements make the world work. Leading involves asking others to make commitments and expecting them to live up to them. If someone does not fulfill his commitment, then the issue is not whether or not they have done the work, but whether their word is worth anything.

Exceptional leaders honor their commitments and hold others to theirs—even for little stuff, like showing up to meetings on time and being prepared.

Our clients have transformed their organizational culture by learning how to make requests and keep promises. They have created cultures of commitment and accountability. Leaders no longer undergo the stress of having to chase others to make sure that tasks are completed. If a request can't be accommodated for some reason, the person who agreed to it comes back and renegotiates.

Organizations with a culture of commitment work better and are more successful than those without. It is that simple.

THOUGHT-PROVOKER

- Do you do what you say you are going to do? Do you keep your promises?
- Do you show up to meetings on time?
- Do you check on others' work rather than manage their promises?
- Do you get caught up in others' excuses and stories?
- Do you expect others to keep their promises and hold them accountable? Or do you just do the work yourself when others don't come through?

Accountability, commitment, and trust deserve reflection and discussion within any organization. They make society and the world work.

Importance (1–5)   ____

Next Actions

EXCEPTIONAL LEADERS ...
Manage the Board

EXCEPTIONAL LEADERS KNOW that members of the board of directors, whether private or public, are key stakeholders in the success of a company. Board relationships need to be managed constructively, recognizing the concerns of board members, particularly in today's regulatory environment.

When a board exercises its management and oversight responsibilities, tensions can develop between company leadership and board members. Exceptional leaders manage this tension and ensure that board members' needs are met while they are powerfully leading the company.

In addition, a successful partnership requires an alignment of values and vision between the board and corporate leadership. This requires that there be a commitment of deep and regular communication on the part of all parties.

Recognizing the importance of a good relationship with the board, exceptional leaders develop relationships with individual board members.

THOUGHT–PROVOKER

- Do you meet informally, one-on-one with board members to establish personal relationships?
- Do you empathize with board members and make efforts to address their concerns?
- Do you solicit others' points of view, seeking to learn as well as communicate?
- Do you clearly, concisely, and regularly communicate with the board, educating them on corporate strategies, issues, and performance, making sure board meeting bring no surprises?
- Do you quickly inform board members about corporate problems that may put them at risk personally and recommend mitigating actions?

CEOs effectively manage relationships with all stakeholders and, in particular, members of the board of directors.

Importance (1–5)   ____

Next Actions

EXCEPTIONAL LEADERS...
Pay Undivided Attention

ALL OF US HAVE BEEN IN another person's office and experienced him or her "timeshare" while conversing with us: checking e-mail, reading and shuffling papers, or even answering the phone What message is that person giving us by doing this? Is effective communication really occurring?

Exceptional Leaders give undivided attention to the person with whom they are conversing. When they do, they are conveying non-verbally that the other person is valuable and that what they have to say is important. This fulfills two basic needs that all of us have; to feel important and to be treated with dignity. Without showing this respect to others, leaders lose considerable respect from others.

Exceptional Leaders understand that not paying undivided attention can lead to breakdowns in understanding and full communications.

THOUGHT-PROVOKER

- How truly effective is your communication with another when you timeshare during a conversation?
- Do you shut off your Blackberry or IPhone during one-on-one and group meetings?
- Are you distracted and do you perform other tasks when on conference calls?
- Do you consciously decide to focus on the other person when the conversation begins?
- Do you set up your work environment so that you can focus, such as by turning off e-mail alarms?
- Do you show respect by truly focusing on what others have to say in the present moment?

Exceptional Leaders don't timeshare in the midst of a conversation with another person. Doing so is just plain rude.

Importance (1–5)   ____

Next Actions

EXCEPTIONAL LEADERS ...
Pick Their Battles

EXCEPTIONAL LEADERS KNOW they can't have everything exactly as they would like. Many competing constituencies with different agendas, needs, and objectives exist within any organization. Each person believes he or she has the right solution from his/her point of view. Compromise, collaboration, taking a firm stand, and simply letting go and not choosing to fight can all be appropriate strategies in a conflict, depending on the circumstances and the stakes involved.

Exceptional leaders know that others must win at times in order for the organization to function effectively. Sometimes the energy and political capital expended may not be worth getting the exact outcome they want.

When they do pick a battle, exceptional leaders do so in light of the circumstances and the ramifications of a battle, knowing that theirs is the right path. They strategize constructively and ethically to get what they want.

In the midst of a battle they are politically astute. They respect others' dignity and needs, and preserve needed relationships for the long term.

THOUGHT-PROVOKER

- Do you get into conflicts over minor issues?
- Do you withdraw to avoid conflicts?
- Do you willingly compromise; knowing that sometimes others need to win and that there is always more than one solution to a problem?
- Do you get into conflicts on matters that are really none of your business?
- When the battle is over, do you focus on the future and refrain from holding the outcome over others, or do you hold a grudge?

Exceptional leaders know that passion for one's agenda is positive. Battles are a part of life, and in business they can lead to positive outcomes.

Importance (1–5) ____

Next Actions

EXCEPTIONAL LEADERS ...
Play Aim Game, Not Blame Game

IT IS EASY TO FIND FAULT. All of us can have negative assessments of what should or should not have been done in a given circumstance. Looking at the past and blaming others, however, is not as productive as looking to the future. No one can change the past.

Exceptional leaders use a "lessons learned" approach and play the aim game rather than the blame game. They create a "blame free" environment. They focus on the future conditions and actions rather than focusing on previous negative events.[4]

Focusing on the future creates clarity and motivates employees. Blaming employees discourages them.

THOUGHT-PROVOKER

Blame Questions

- What is the problem, and why do you have it?
- What is limiting or preventing you from getting what you want?
- Whose fault is it?

Aim Questions

- What is your desired outcome?
- How will you know when you get there?
- What actions can you take to get where you want to be?
- What have you learned about yourself from the situation?

Exceptional leaders focus on the future, which they have some control over, rather than the past, which they can neither change nor control.

Importance (1–5)   ____

Next Actions

EXCEPTIONAL LEADERS ...
Show Up

FOR EMPLOYEES TO BE fully engaged and committed, leaders have to be engaged with employees. This includes showing up.

Exceptional leaders are visible and interested in how the people in the organization are doing. They make time for "face time" with small groups and individuals in order to convey their message.

Leaders express interest. They encourage others. They show appreciation. They celebrate accomplishments. These are all the actions of an inspiring leader.

Leaders of large organizations show up personally at least two levels down from them in the hierarchy. They use other means to be visible throughout the rest of the organization.

Exceptional leaders learn to present effectively. They learn how to inspire groups through their presentations. They know how to rally the troops.

THOUGHT-PROVOKER

- When did you last have an intensive, one-on-one conversation with an employee other than your direct reports?
- Do you express genuine interest in what others in the organization do?
- Do you personally encourage others?
- Do you celebrate the successes of others with them?
- Can you give effective, inspiring presentations?

Exceptional leaders get out of their offices to connect with employees and inspire them to be their best.

Importance (1–5) _____

Next Actions

EXCEPTIONAL LEADERS ...
Take the Blame

SOME COMMITTEES ARE WONDERFUL because they are risk free. Members can take credit for successes and no one person is responsible for failures. The question is "does not having more than one person responsible for the outcome of an initiative lead to the best results?" The answer is no. Committees can't lead: individuals can. That is the reason corporate boards with capable people chose to hire executives to lead the company rather than doing it themselves. No oligarchies in history have ever succeeded for very long.

Leaders are willing to take risks, take action and be responsible for outcomes. They have the courage of their convictions and they meet their commitments. They are willing to take the blame when something does not go as expected. They don't shift the blame to others or make excuses. This does not mean that they have to fall on their sword. It does mean that they are willing to lead, make tough decisions, and be accountable, admit they failed, learn, and move on with confidence.

Leaders should also expect others to be accountable and willing to take the blame for those things that go wrong within their area of responsibility. They don't tolerate excuses or blame shifting. Accountability provides the energy to make sure that outcomes are clearly defined and are successful.

THOUGHT-PROVOKER

- Are your accountabilities absolutely clear to you and to others?
- Do you honor your commitments?
- When things do go wrong (and they will), do you take responsibility or do you make excuses?
- Do you hold others to account?

Exceptional leaders take responsibility and hold themselves and others accountable for outcomes.

Importance (1–5) _____

Next Actions

EXCEPTIONAL LEADERS ...
Take Time for Themselves

LEADING COMPLEX ORGANIZATIONS REQUIRES responding to multiple stakeholders and expending a large amount of energy over an extended period. Only then will most leaders achieve organizational objectives and success.

For many leaders, however, incurring extended periods of reaction and response to others takes its toll. When leaders don't take time for themselves, they lose effectiveness, get burned out, and can even become physically sick.

The stress associated with not taking care of yourself can create circumstances where you do not behave at your best. This can have a negative impact on those around you and reduce your effectiveness.

Exceptional leaders take the necessary downtime to rejuvenate and recharge their batteries.

THOUGHT-PROVOKER

- Are you exhausted from pursuing your goals and meeting the demands of others?
- Is it time to restructure and reprioritize in order to take care of you?
- Do you focus on the needs of others so much that you don't focus on your own?
- Do you regularly schedule leisure time to rejuvenate?
- Is it time to take a Blackberry-free vacation?

Exceptional leaders take care of themselves so they can be available for others and be fully energized to lead effectively.

Importance (1–5)   ____

Next Actions

EXCEPTIONAL LEADERS ...
Masterfully Manage Change

LEADERS INITIATE CHANGE in order to meet current and future demands of their organizations. Exceptional leaders manage change and its impact on people and the organization.

Whenever an important change occurs, a natural psychological process occurs which we call a transition. Change is external. A transition is the internal process that an individual goes through. Transitions have four phases:

Phase One—Denial
A person experiences disbelief and denial—the change does not seem real, and the person can deny that it will affect them emotionally.

Phase Two—Resistance
Negative emotions, such as anger and anxiety, emerge. Resistance is often grounded in fear. This can lead to unproductive behavior: complaining, inactivity, and stalling out on implementation.

Phase Three—Exploration. The person's focus shifts toward the future, and they begin to see possibilities and opportunities.

Phase Four—Recommitment
The person becomes recommitted and comfortable with a new beginning.

The leader's role is to help others accelerate through the transition process.

Leaders can go through their own transition process prior to initiating an organizational change, and may fail to recognize that they are ahead of their employees. Then they expect others to simply "get over it."

Leaders can help their employees in the change process and help people accelerate through it.

When others are in denial and disbelief, leaders communicate masterfully and repeatedly.

When others are in resistance, they listen. They allow others to express their concerns, and then they address implementation issues based on relevant feedback. Informal discussion, focus groups, and surveys can be helpful during this phase.

Once employees feel that they have been heard, they are ready to explore options for creating a new future. Leaders facilitate that process.

When a shared future is agreed upon, associates are ready to recommit to the new beginning. They celebrate.

THOUGHT-PROVOKER

- Do you know when you are in a transition?
- Do you know where you and your associates are in the change process?
- Do you communicate relentlessly when others are in denial?
- Do you listen deeply when others are in resistance?
- Do you facilitate when others are exploring options?
- Do you celebrate the recommitment?
- Or, having gone through the change process yourself, do you tell others to just get over it?

Exceptional leaders help others move through the change process, maximizing organizational performance and profitability.

Importance (1–5) ____

Next Actions

UNDERSTAND CULTURES

CULTURE
VALUES
BELIEFS
STORIES

EXCEPTIONAL LEADERS ...
Understand Cultures

EXCEPTIONAL LEADERS LEARN TO understand the cultures of the groups with whom they deal. In The Leadership Mastery Map, the collective interior subjective (lower left quadrant) should be taken into consideration in all decisions and evaluations.

This domain consists of shared subjective beliefs and values. It is what individuals hold in common within a particular group. This could include a department, a company, a company or an ethnic or corporate group.

Executives who focus only on the transactional commercial aspects of a business (lower right quadrant) can be blindsided by the important dynamics of culture. You see many examples of this when large change initiatives, such as mergers, are unsuccessful.

If a leader only looks at the commercial aspects and ignores the cultural dynamics—the shared beliefs among employees or customers ("what our customers want") and values ("what is really important to us")—significant resistance sometimes emerges, which could prove fatal to a change initiative.

THOUGHT-PROVOKER

- What are the core beliefs and values of the organizational culture you find yourself in?
- When you make decisions, do you take these into consideration?
- Do you really know how groups will react in given situations, whether employees, customers, or consumers? If not, how do you know that you will make the right decision?
- Are your core values compatible with the values of the group you find yourself aligned with? What specific examples make you confident of this?

Exceptional leaders know that a firm understanding of the cultural dynamics of the groups they interact with is essential to effective business decisions and evaluations.

Importance (1–5)   ____

Next Actions

EXCEPTIONAL LEADERS ...
Are Candid

HOW MANY TIMES do you fail to initiate crucial conversations to avoid anticipated reactions from others? Exceptional leaders not only see the elephant in the room, they talk about it.

In their book *Winning*, Jack and Suzy Welch advocate being candid.   Hidden agendas, unspoken truths or assessments, and avoided confrontations rob an organization of the dialog necessary for it to be successful. Only when leaders engage in rigorous conversations can the needed issues be surfaced and addressed. [6]

Exceptional leaders know that it is possible to be candid yet constructive, to be candid yet recognize the feelings of others, to be candid and still have others like and respect them.

THOUGHT-PROVOKER

- Can you be constructively candid with those around you?
- What conversations are you avoiding?
- Who are you avoiding?
- What would be the benefits for you and your organization if everyone talked about the crucial things needed to be successful—even though such conversations may be painful?
- What conversation can you have today that will put things that need to be addressed on the table?

Exceptional leaders communicate fully, even when the truth hurts.

Importance (1–5) ____

Next Actions

EXCEPTIONAL LEADERS ...
Are Open to New Ideas

EXCEPTIONAL LEADERS KNOW that their reactions to new ideas will either encourage or discourage innovation and creativity.

Some leaders respond to new ideas in ways that turn people off, becoming negative when new ideas are presented: "It won't work" or "We tried that before." Or they instantly come up with other ideas to shut down the presenter. Worse yet, they may take credit for new ideas after initially responding negatively.

Exceptional leaders respond to new ideas in ways that support others' innovation and creativity. A good example is the President of HEB Grocery, who did not think that the Central Market, a high end grocery store concept, would work. Nevertheless, he allowed his people to open a pilot store. He found out that his initial reaction was wrong. Central Market has become very successful.

When leaders discourage innovation and creativity, people tend to check their brains at the door. Exceptional leaders are open to new ideas and foster creativity and innovation at every opportunity.

THOUGHT-PROVOKER

- Do you have a new idea generation engine in your organization?
- What processes and systems are in place to foster new ideas?
- Do you hire and nurture leading-edge thinkers to ensure that your organization innovates when the time is right?
- How do you respond to others who suggest new ideas?
- Do you facilitate and encourage their creative thinking, or do you ignore, discourage, or dismiss them?

In today's era of accelerated change, new ideas truly are the engine that drives an organization's survival and success.

Importance (1–5) _____

Next Actions

EXCEPTIONAL LEADERS ...
Are Outrageously Positive

RESEARCH HAS SHOWN that being positive and reacting positively yields better results in every situation. Exceptional leaders know that being positive pays big dividends. Moods are contagious.

Some leaders default to what's wrong. Their first response to new ideas is "no." They sort for the negatives—what's wrong, what's flawed, what's missing, what's not working. This approach has some value. However, it is valuable only after the positive has been mined and in the context of consciously playing the devil's advocate.

In looking for what is right, what could work, and what is working, the exceptional leader balances out the negative and critical approaches. The ratio should be five or six positives to each negative.

THOUGHT-PROVOKER

- How do you initially react: positively or negatively?
- Are you optimistic and upbeat? Do you know that, as you are a leader, others are intensely attuned to your attitudes and moods?
- Do your attitudes and moods create a can-do culture?
- Do you focus solely or first on the negatives?
- Do your reactions shut people down, or do you respond in ways that motivate and bring out the best from your employees?
- How do others respond to your communications? Are they motivated or de-motivated?

Exceptional leaders know that by being positive, they breed an upbeat, productive, and motivated workforce.

Importance (1–5) _____

Next Actions

EXCEPTIONAL LEADERS ...
Are Socially Aware

EXCEPTIONAL LEADERS LISTEN intently and pick up empathetically on unspoken and intuitive cues from others. They grasp the other person's perspective and emotions. This allows for more effective communication and connections with others. [11]

Sometimes we don't pick up on cues, such as when to end a conversation. Someone can give nonverbal cues that they want to end the conversation, and yet we keep on talking. We are unaware of the other person's internal state.

Having a sense of what is going on with another person, generally and in one-on-one communication, is a foundational skill for influencing others. Sensing how others feel is an aspect of being emotionally intelligent.

Sometimes, in order to verify what is going on with another person and not just assume the role of mind-reader, we simply need to ask. We can then fashion our communication to be effective.

THOUGHT-PROVOKER

- Do you have an intuitive sense of how others feel? Are you getting the truth?
- Do you see how others respond nonverbally to your communications and to situations?
- Do you look for body language, facial expressions, and what's behind the words?
- Do you inquire of others as to what is really going on in their minds, expressing empathy and understanding?
- Do you know when to end a conversation?

Exceptional leaders have the perceptual acuity to see what others think and feel and they can adjust their communications accordingly.

Importance (1–5)   _____

Next Actions

EXCEPTIONAL LEADERS ...
Are Transparent

TRANSPARENT LEADERS LIVE their values. Those with whom they work see an authentic openness about their beliefs, their feelings, and most importantly, their actions. This transparency allows for integrity and trust-building.

Exceptional leaders are willing to let themselves and others be human—what you see is what you get. When we see our leaders as human we tend to trust them more. When leaders hold themselves up to being beyond mere mortals, then there is a lack of trust.

Transparency also means that a leader's actions, and the reasons behind the actions, are obvious and known to everyone. There are no hidden agendas. There is clarity on everyone's part as to what the leader and the organization is up to.

When leaders are open and authentic, they are attractive and can inspire and energize others.

THOUGHT-PROVOKER

- How open are you? Are your actions and motivations apparent to others? Or perhaps, do they see manipulation?
- Are you willing to appear imperfect, admitting mistakes and faults?
- Do you confront unethical behavior in others rather than turning a blind eye?
- Are you willing to express your excitement and joys as well as your sadness and frustration?
- What part of you needs to be revealed for others to know how exceptional you are?

With exceptional leaders, what you see is what you get.

Importance (1–5)   _____

Next Actions

EXCEPTIONAL LEADERS...
Build Powerful Teams

A TEAM IS A GROUP OF INTERDEPENDENT individuals committed to achieving a common objective. The team's success depends on the contribution of each member. Exceptional leaders build powerful teams by finding the right people for the team and insuring that everyone on the team is focused on a common objective, aligned with each other on roles and responsibilities, and communicating effectively.

Team members must trust each other to perform their respective roles. This means that team members are reliable and competent. Team members collaborate with each other and fully express their individual views. This means that there must be a certain level of comfort with constructive conflict.

High performance teams also focus on each team member's development. They understand that for the team to continuously improve and meet what should be demanding objectives, team members need to be learning and growing.

Exceptional Leaders orchestrate all the dynamics of team performance, insuring that the team members' collective efforts achieve the agreed-upon objectives.

THOUGHT–PROVOKER

- What part of you needs to be revealed for others to know how exceptional you are? Do you truly have the right people on your team?
- Do team members personally know each other? Do they trust each other?
- Do team members know each other's strengths and improvement areas?
- Is your team focused and aligned on a common objective?
- Do teams collaborate effectively together, insuring that all views are expressed?
- Do you as a team leader inspire and motivate your team?

Exceptional Leaders keep teams on track and achieve outstanding results.

Importance (1–5)   ____

Next Actions

EXCEPTIONAL LEADERS....
Build Trust

TRUST IS A VITAL COMPONENT of successful leadership and successful organizations. Exceptional leaders build trust, and if trust breaks down, they rebuild it.

Trust has four key elements. Analyzing these elements can uncover how trust is built and rebuilt.

You are going to trust someone if you perceive them to be:

- **Truthful** - The words that come out of their mouth are aligned with what they are thinking and what they know to be the truth. They are sincere.

- **Caring** - If we perceive that someone does not care, it is unlikely that we will trust them. Politicians know this.

- **Reliable** - They do what they say they are going to do on time, every time.

- **Competent** - You see them as capable of doing their work. Consider tandem sky diving with an instructor whom you don't perceive as competent.

Exceptional leaders are truthful, caring, reliable, and competent. You can trust them. They rebuild trust by analyzing where trust has broken down and talk about it. They then take actions to rebuild trust.

THOUGHT-PROVOKER

- Are you trustworthy? If not, what element do you need to work on?
- Do you work in an organization that permeates trust?
- Do your employees, vendors, customers and other stakeholders trust you? Do you trust them?
- When trust has broken down are you willing to have a conversation about rebuilding trust?

Exceptional Leaders work hard at building and maintaining trust. They know if they don't, in the long run, they will fail.

Importance (1–5) _____

Next Actions

EXCEPTIONAL LEADERS ...
Celebrate Successes

HIGHLY AMBITIOUS AND energized leaders can often overlook people's need to celebrate and acknowledge success.

Everyone exhausts themselves to get to the top of the mountain, and the leader immediately points to the next mountain to climb. This can be de-motivating, causing employees to be less than enthusiastic about working on the next big thing.

Exceptional leaders know that, in order to keep others consistently motivated, they must find ways and take time to celebrate.

Celebrating creates *esprit* and good feelings among a group of employees. They are then ready to tackle the next big thing.

THOUGHT-PROVOKER

- Do you take the time to celebrate?
- What have the people in your organization done lately that deserves to be celebrated?
- Do you have celebrations when an employee puts in an extra effort?
- In looking at your goals for yourself and others, have you determined how you will celebrate reaching them? Have you told others how everyone will celebrate?

Exceptional leaders are cheerleaders for others and celebrate successes.

Importance (1–5)   ____

Next Actions

EXCEPTIONAL LEADERS ...
Create Fans

TO BE SUCCESSFUL, leaders have to have people who will be advocates for them. There are times when individuals who are high performers and change agents can be blindsided by others' negative views of them. Sometimes it makes the difference between whether or not they survive in a job.

In large organizations, the political dynamics can result in meetings where others, for whatever reason, express negative views about a particular individual. The negative opinions may stick when others are neutral and are not disposed to defend them.

Exceptional leaders know that they need to create fans and advocates, particularly if they are a change agent, because others may resist their changes and complain about them. They are careful to build multiple positive relationships with their boss, peers, and direct reports in the midst of accomplishing great things.

THOUGHT-PROVOKER

- To what degree do you balance doing your work and focusing on the objective of building relationships?
- Do you purposely cultivate relationships with peers and all those impacted by your actions?
- Do you do a risk analysis related to your initiatives so that you can mitigate unintended consequences?
- Do you know which of your colleagues would defend each other should you criticize them?
- Do you support others in their objectives and concerns?
- When issues arise, do you defend your colleagues from unjustified criticism?

Exceptional leaders create fans in the midst of meeting the challenges of today's business environment.

Importance (1–5)   ____

Next Actions

EXCEPTIONAL LEADERS ...
Cull Bad Apples

THERE IS AN ADAGE that "one bad apple spoils the basket."

Research has shown that teams perform at the level of the lowest performing person, not the average or the top performer. The low performer brings the others down. Their attitude and behaviors are infectious.

You may have experienced bad apples on a team or within a work group. While they are usually a very small percentage of any work group, they can have a big impact. They usually fall into one of three types.

- **The Depressive Pessimists**...the person who puts a negative spin on everything. They sort the world for negatives and communicate it to everyone.

- **The Jerk**...the person who is abusive to others. They put people down. They discount others' contributions. They cause others to feel either hurt, angry or both.

- **The Slacker**...the person who does not do their share of the work. They look for ways to avoid work. They don't honor their commitments.

Exceptional leaders deal with bad apples by counseling them and if there is no change, letting them go. This way they can upgrade the quality of the team and its performance.

THOUGHT-PROVOKER

- Have you assessed the performance of your team lately?
- Do you know how individual team members are impacting the performance of the overall team?
- Have you or your managers been willing to make the tough decisions needed to increase the team's performance?
- What conversations can you have today that will impact the productivity of your teams?

Exceptional leaders cultivate top performers and top performance. When this does not occur, they do something about it.

Importance (1–5)   ____

Next Actions

EXCEPTIONAL LEADERS ...
Demonstrate They Care

ONE OF THE PRIMARY reasons employees quit or don't perform is that they think that their leaders don't care about them.   When leaders are perceived as not caring, employees feel used rather than led.   Research shows that employees quit their boss rather than the company.

Another dynamic associated with caring is trust.   If you perceive that someone does not really care about you, are you going to trust them? Leaders who show they care are more likely to be trusted.

One can think of political leaders who demonstrate caring, particularly in moments of crisis. They are more trusted and admired.

With today's critical shortage of talent, exceptional leaders know that a key part of their job includes seeing others as more than instruments to get things done. They see the whole person, not just their role or function.

THOUGHT-PROVOKER

- Do you look for opportunities to show that you care, for instance when employees face a personal crisis?
- Do you take steps to ensure that the workload is distributed fairly and that top performers are not overloaded and overwhelmed?
- Do you check in with others in a genuinely caring way, rather than just saying, "How are you?"
- Can you connect with your employees' personal lives at some level, so they know you see them as fellow human beings?
- When did you last connect with a fellow employee— really connected at the heart level?

Exceptional leaders know that employees who know that their leaders care about them will perform better and make the company successful.

Importance (1–5) _____

Next Actions

EXCEPTIONAL LEADERS ...
Display a Sense of Humor

EVERYONE KNOWS THAT NONE of us is getting out of this alive, so why take things so seriously? Many great leaders have had a terrific sense of humor during good times and bad. These include Abraham Lincoln, John F. Kennedy, Winston Churchill, and Ronald Reagan.

Not taking yourself or external events so seriously, even in dire situations, releases stress. Others around you become more at ease. Scientific studies have shown that moods are contagious and a leader's good mood can motivate their subordinates. Seeing the humor in situations creates positive feelings. Positive moods generate positive action. Negative moods generate negative action or inaction.

Exceptional leaders know that others take their cues from them, and they act accordingly. They can be funny when the time is right.

THOUGHT-PROVOKER

- As a leader, are you continually aware of your mood?
- Can you see how your mood impacts others?
- Are you able to inject humor into tense situations?
- Can you see the humor in your own actions when needed?
- Do you see how having a sense of humor in what appear to be important or ominous situations can actually improve others' abilities to address the situation?

For exceptional leaders, when things get tough, the tough lighten up and then get going.

Importance (1–5)   _____

Next Actions

EXCEPTIONAL LEADERS ...
Display Masterful Interpersonal Skills

AS A LEADER, you are at risk if you do not master interpersonal skills.   In today's corporate environment, any employee can make complaints to a Sarbanes-Oxley hotline or human resources. Because of potential liabilities to the corporation, managers may be considered guilty simply because a complaint is made. The burden of proof will be on the manager rather than the one who voiced the complaint. Because feelings are involved, it can be very difficult to defend oneself.

High performing leaders with millions of dollars of responsibility who make significant contributions to a corporation can unknowingly place their career at risk simply by hurting the feelings of a clerk.

With social media and internet reviews making all complaints easy to air, leaders may find themselves having to explain publicly and apologize for their interpersonal mis-steps.

Because of this and because it is simply the right thing to do, it is imperative that exceptional leaders be masterful in their interpersonal relations, respecting the dignity of everyone with whom they come in contact.

THOUGHT-PROVOKER

- How sensitive are you to how you your words might impact others?
- Do you know and use the components of emotional intelligence?
- Do you respect the dignity of those with whom you work?
- Do you know how to avoid getting your buttons pushed and communicating inappropriately?

Exceptional leaders treat everyone with dignity while effectively leading and coordinating action.

Importance (1–5)   _____

Next Actions

EXCEPTIONAL LEADERS ...
Don't Drive Others Crazy

YOU MAY HAVE SEEN leaders drive others crazy. No one intentionally sets out to drive others crazy—and yet it happens. Studies show that normal people can become almost psychotic when they are caught in a double-bind situation. [7] Here is how to create the double-bind:

First, make someone dependent on you for his welfare and security. Then give them a strong directive ("Increase production"). Then give them another strong directive that contradicts the first ("Reduce costs").Then refuse to talk about the inconsistency ("I don't want to hear about your problems. Just get it done."). It also helps to say that you have an open door policy.

At times, leaders don't realize that they create double-bind situations for their employees. Sometimes double-binds cascade down the hierarchy, getting more bizarre as they descend. This occurs often during the budgeting process.

Another type of double-bind happens when demands conflict with one's internal values. Finding oneself stuck in a situation that conflicts with one's values can be debilitating, to say the least.

Some external circumstances, such as the need to increase prices to be profitable at the same time your competitors lower their prices, create a double-bind situation. These kinds of situations induce incredible stress and drive people crazy.

Exceptional leaders can see when they create a double-bind for others and also when they get caught in one themselves. They take strong initiative to have productive conversations that restore sanity to a situation.

 THOUGHT-PROVOKER

- Think about the demands that currently face you. Do they conflict?
- Do you analyze your stress and bring what is really causing it to the surface?
- Are you willing to engage aggressively in productive conversations that highlight the conflict and work toward resolving and/or prioritizing competing demands?
- As a leader, are you on the lookout for when you create a double-bind for others?
- Are you open and available for others to bring such situations to your attention?

The stress caused by contradictory demands causes suffering and can put you in the hospital.

Importance (1–5)   _____

Next Actions

EXCEPTIONAL LEADERS ...
Don't Shame Others

SHAME IS THE STRONG EMOTION that comes from the perceived injury to one's reputation. This can include being shown as incompetent, erroneous, or powerless. It can produce anger and resentment and will not soon be forgotten.

Exceptional leaders go out of their way to avoid shaming others. They watch their behavior in meetings and deal with issues constructively; making sure the dignity of others is preserved even in the midst of conflict.

They also watch the "reply all" e-mails. Copying everyone under the sun when sending a critical e-mail to someone can have devastating effects, including escalating issues unnecessarily.

THOUGHT-PROVOKER

- Do you personally attack people and their ideas in meetings?
- Do you call them out on their mistakes?
- If you get an e-mail that triggers you, do you wait to respond until you have calmed down?
- Do you pick up the phone when someone appears to be hurt by an e-mail or you have something emotionally charged to say?

Exceptional leaders are able to constructively communicate everything they need to without shaming others.

Importance (1–5)   _____

Next Actions

EXCEPTIONAL LEADERS...
Do Not Tolerate Communication Triangles

A COMMUNICATION TRIANGLE occurs when one person complains or gossips to a second person about a third person.

Exceptional leaders understand the cultural damage that results when triangulating is allowed. It is unacceptable to get something off the chest by complaining to one person about another. Communication triangles pollute the culture of an organization with unresolved complaints and gossip. It is a symptom of powerlessness and serves no useful purpose.

The solution requires a culture where employees are encouraged to confront one another openly and constructively when issues arise. Exceptional leaders set the example by constructively confronting those who have the power to make changes rather than complaining to those who don't.

No team or department can function effectively with a lot of back biting and gossip. This includes an executive group. It is totally unproductive and de-motivating. When this does occur the leader must do something to stop it.

We have found the collective formulation of written guidelines by members of a group can be very helpful.

THOUGHT-PROVOKER

- Do you gossip or complain about others behind their backs?
- Do you listen to others' complaints when you do not have the power to do anything about them?
- Do you foster a culture of openness by encouraging others to constructively and directly address issues they might have with others rather than simply complain?
- Do you encourage employees to assess what they have control over and what they do not?
- Do you encourage them to take action over what they can control and not to complain about what they don't?

Organizations that are open and that encourage constructive confrontation rather than powerless complaining are more successful.

Importance (1–5) ____

Next Actions

EXCEPTIONAL LEADERS ...
Encourage Others

EXCEPTIONAL LEADERS KNOW that how and what they communicate influences employee performance. Knowing this, they encourage others in their work. To encourage means to express enthusiastic confidence in another's ability to accomplish something or to prevail under difficult circumstances.

This seems like a simple idea, and it is. Encouragement is also extraordinarily effective in getting the best out of others. Saying to someone, "You can do it" or "I believe in you" declares the future for them and provides a catalyst for the energy to accomplish and to overcome.

Look at any great sports team, and you will see players, team leaders, and coaches encouraging each other to excel. They give each other high-fives for great plays. They keep each other's passion and mood upbeat, even in the face of setbacks, by encouraging each other.

Parents encourage children in their endeavors; leaders encourage employees in theirs.

THOUGHT-PROVOKER

- When did you last express confidence in someone's ability to accomplish something?
- Do you wait until the performance review to give others positive feedback on their work?
- When did you last give someone a sincere "attaboy" or "attagirl"?
- When did you last ask a direct report what they do to encourage their employees to do and be their best? When do you encourage them?
- Do you declare the possibilities for others, thus creating a successful future?

Exceptional leaders inspire by encouraging others to succeed.

Importance (1–5) _____

Next Actions

EXCEPTIONAL LEADERS ...
Encourage the Millennium Generation

THE MILLENNIUM GENERATION (those born between 1980 and 2000) can be both a challenge and an opportunity. How do you deal with employees who operate quite differently from you?

Members of the Millennium Generation are constantly in contact with their network of friends and colleagues through text messaging. They blog about anything and everything. They self-organize into networks by using technology. They use online creation and collaboration tools such as Wikipedia to partner with others to create knowledge. They time-share in meetings with laptops, phones and tablets as they did in the classroom.

The Millennials watched as their parents were laid off, and the traditional contract between companies and employees was broken. They have also seen their parents make great sacrifices for their jobs. This has caused them to have a more personal perspective on work. They may be more committed to their work, but not the company.

Rather than resisting and forbidding these trends, exceptional leaders engage younger employees and discover ways to incorporate new ways of operating to increase the value of their work and the organization. Leaders should be flexible and willing to negotiate new ways of working.

THOUGHT-PROVOKER

- How do you react when you see young workers doing new things with technology that you don't understand?
- Do you assume that new technology wastes time and reduces productivity?
- To what degree have you really tried to understand the technological mentality of younger workers?
- Do you partner with early adopters to discover new ways of working while setting appropriate boundaries when needed?
- Do you make adjustments in work schedules and demands to accommodate this new reality?

Exceptional leaders recognize the contribution that younger workers make to an organization and encourage them, when appropriate, by accepting new ways of working.

Importance (1–5) _____

Next Actions

EXCEPTIONAL LEADERS ...
Express Appreciation

RESEARCH HAS CONSISTENTLY SHOWN "lack of appreciation" to be one of the key issues employees have with management.

This complaint also shows up when leaders use multi-rater feedback instruments to measure other people's perceptions of their leadership capabilities.

Employees are satisfied and motivated when they receive acknowledgement and positive regard from their leaders.

Employee engagement is most impacted by the direct supervisor and appreciation can go a long way in causing employees to feel connected to the organization.

Exceptional leaders take the time to express and show appreciation frequently, both with groups and individuals.

THOUGHT-PROVOKER

- When did you last receive a sincere expression of appreciation from your boss? How did it feel and to what degree did it motivate you?
- Identify three key people in your work life, perhaps peers or subordinates. Think about their gifts. What strengths do they bring to the job?
- In what ways could you express appreciation for who they are and the work that they do?

Decide to show appreciation. Think about the words you will use. Even write them down. Decide whether to communicate your appreciation in writing or orally. Make the time to do it.

Importance (1–5)   ____

Next Actions

EXCEPTIONAL LEADERS ...
Foster Employee Engagement

AN ENGAGED EMPLOYEE is motivated, finds personal worth in their work, and is committed to the accomplishment of goals. These employees consider contribution to the organization to be essential to achieving organizational goals. Exceptional leaders know that effective leadership is the key to developing and maintaining employee engagement.

Research in the U.S. shows that 29 percent of employees are engaged in their work, 55 percent are not engaged and 15 percent are actively not engaged.[8] Research and common sense show that companies with more engaged employees are more successful. Productivity and innovation runs higher. Customer relations fare better. The organizational culture is more positive.

THOUGHT-PROVOKER

- Are your employees enthusiastic about what they do, or are they resigned to their jobs, going through the motions and acting powerless?
- Do your employees have all of the training and resources needed to do their jobs effectively?
- Do you, as a leader, project enthusiasm and tell employees how they personally play vital roles in the company's future success?
- Do you know your employees—especially their goals, their stressors, what excites them, and how they each define success?
- Are you alert to counterproductive behavior or negative attitudes? Do you take action to make improvements?

Exceptional leaders commit to fostering employee enthusiasm about employees' jobs and the organization.

Importance (1–5) _____

Next Actions

EXCEPTIONAL LEADERS ...
Invite the Truth

TO BE EFFECTIVE, leaders must know what really happens within their organization.

Inherent in the nature of organizations and individuals is a tendency toward fear. This fear causes employees to withhold bad news, lest their leaders hold them responsible.

Some leaders' negative reactions to bad news can lead employees to either soft-peddle the truth or simply not communicate it. This reluctance to deliver bad news causes the leader to be blind as to what is really going on—which provides a sure path to failure as a leader. [11]

Some leaders invite the truth and react to communications in a way that drives out the natural fear that exists in most organizations. They create strategies and develop competencies that build a culture of trust. They know what is going on, both the good news and the bad news, and can therefore respond appropriately to the needs of the business.

THOUGHT-PROVOKER

- Are you getting the truth?
- Are you aware of the natural tendency of employees to "put a positive slant on things"?
- Does your personal style create a culture of trust by empowering others to provide all the information, both good and bad?
- How do you react to bad news? Do you shoot the messenger?
- What systems can you put in place to ensure that you get the truth or all of the information that you need to be successful?

Exceptional leaders know that successful organizations keep fear at a minimum, and foster the natural flow of good *and* bad news.

Importance (1–5)   _____

Next Actions

EXCEPTIONAL LEADERS ...
Listen with Intention

EXCEPTIONAL LEADERS KNOW that listening is as much a choice as it is a skill. When they decide to listen with intention, they are able to get all of the information they need. One can listen with a learning mind-set or a judging mind-set.

Learners remain open for new information and are slow to come down with an opinion or judgment while listening. They have the intention of surfacing everything the other person has to say. They ask many questions to fully explore the other person's thought processes before responding.

Listening with a judging mind-set means a person has no real intention to listen. One's mind is already made up or energized to come to a judgment quickly and communicate it.

Good listeners recognize that others have needs. The need for others to express themselves may be more important than the content of what they are saying. Attentive listeners let people speak their piece, recognizing that at times it is more important to preserve relationships than be right.

Exceptional leaders decide to listen. By doing so, they get all of the information needed to fully understand what others want to say.

THOUGHT-PROVOKER

- Do you ask questions to facilitate another person's communication before you respond?
- Do you reflect back the feelings you heard as well as the words to the person who expressed them?
- Do you notice an internal energy that may compel you to interrupt others before they have finished talking? Can you decide to not react, but to fully listen with intention?
- Do you interrupt others, not letting them fully communicate their point?
- Can you acknowledge another person's need to be heard?

Then again, you could be like one manager who said, "One thing that really bothers me is when people keep talking while I am trying to interrupt them."

Importance (1–5) _____

Next Actions

EXCEPTIONAL LEADERS ...
Reduce Power Differences

ARE YOU GETTING THE STRAIGHT SCOOP from your people? Are they willing to vigorously argue with you? Or do people always defer to your views?

In his book, Outliers, Malcolm Gladwell notes that most airline accidents are due to pilot error, and that the power differential in the cockpit between the pilot and co-pilot has a significant impact on the performance of the crew. If the co-pilot feels significantly less powerful than the pilot, he will be less likely to speak up when the pilot sounds certain about decisions that he questions. Disastrous errors can then occur.

Other psychological research shows that in controlled circumstances those who are in authority can actually get others to override their moral foundations and do things that would be unthinkable to them. Experiments have been conducted showing that subjects will administer a lethal electrical shock to others simply because someone in authority tells them to do so. What this means is that the differential in authority, i.e., power, has a huge influence on how people communicate and behave.

In today's rough economic times, leaders have to make hard decisions. Exceptional leaders know they need all the input they can get to ensure that they are making the best decisions. This means creating a climate that actually reduces their status and power, so that others will have the wherewithal to speak up and voice their views.

Exceptional leaders must actively encourage forthright communications and, at times, intense conflict in order to get the best decisions possible.

 THOUGHT–PROVOKER

- How do you reduce the trappings of your "office" in order to get full communications?
- In what ways do you encourage and make it comfortable for others to disagree with you, or do they feel consequences for voicing difference?
- How would your team rate you on your willingness for others to challenge your plans and ideas?

Exceptional leaders know they need to reduce the power differential so that they can foster others' forthright input and avoid disasters, just like pilots do in the cockpit.

Importance (1–5) ____

Next Actions

EXCEPTIONAL LEADERS ...
See People as People

THIS MIGHT SOUND STRANGE, but sometimes we don't see people as people. The most personal example is when we are stressed out by traffic. Do you, like most of us, objectify other drivers, not really seeing them as people, as human beings like you who are just trying to get through this world as best they can?

Anytime we find ourselves being critical or judgmental, we shift into this "thing" mind-set and lose touch with the humanity of others—as well as our own humanity. When we do this, only negative and unintended outcomes arise.

In leading, particularly when we are under stress, we can see others as instruments to get things done, rather than as what they really are: people.

You can be an effective leader, even being critical and demanding, when you have a compassionate mind-set. It is not so much our behavior that makes the difference, but our state of mind.

When we speak and act from a compassionate way of being, we can create the culture we want and accomplish great things. We must continually be aware of our mind-set to ensure that we don't objectify others.

THOUGHT-PROVOKER

- Do you find that others communicate with you in ways that diminish your humanity? How do you feel at those times? How connected and motivated are you then?
- Do you sometimes see others as merely objects to get things done?
- Can you have compassion in the midst of pressing matters?
- Do you see everyone as human, or do you see only those you love as human?

Exceptional leaders continually keep in touch with their own humanity, as well as the humanity of others. We are all doing the best we can.

Importance (1–5)   ____

Next Actions

EXCEPTIONAL LEADERS ...
Support Allies

WE HAVE TALKED ABOUT CREATING FANS. This time we are talking about creating allies. An ally is someone who you align with to achieve a common goal. One would think that all departments and peers would be allies around the success of a company, and behave accordingly. However, sometimes internal competition fosters behavior that looks very different and can actually diminish a company's success.

An example would be manufacturing plants that do not share best practices in order to "beat" each other, or departments working at cross purposes due to their managers' competitiveness. Neither example is in the best interest of the company.

Exceptional leaders know that success will come more from creating allies rather than creating enemies. They seek and negotiate alignments with other entities so that each can achieve common objectives.

THOUGHT-PROVOKER

- Who are you allied with in your company?
- Do you compete with your peers, or do you build alliances with them?
- With whom are you competing and is it really serving you and the organization's interests to do so?
- With what department, or other organizational entity, do you need to build a deeper alliance?
- How can you help your peers achieve their objectives?

Exceptional leaders build alliances by seeking out others to identify and achieve common objectives.

Importance (1–5) _____

Next Actions

EXCEPTIONAL LEADERS ...
Walk Their Talk

CREDIBILITY IS ESSENTIAL for trust. Trust is essential for exceptional leadership. When leaders say they are going to do something, they must do it, and when they say they are not going to do something, they should not do it.

How many of us have heard stories of leaders communicating that nothing will change during a merger, that the merger is only an investment relationship, that jobs will not be impacted? Then massive changes, including layoffs, take place. Credibility is blown from the get-go.

Another example of leaders not walking their talk comes from the conduct of the employee survey. Employees are solicited for their opinions with an expectation that results will be made public and action will be taken on justifiable criticism. The survey is taken, but no follow-up reporting or visible action materializes. It would be better not to carry out a survey at all than to undermine leadership credibility.

THOUGHT-PROVOKER

Do you say things to others, trying to be nice, while unintentionally creating positive expectations that certain things will happen—and then you don't follow through?

Do you communicate slippery promises? For example, do you say, "I will try to do such and such"? Do others perceive it as a commitment when you don't?

Do you hold yourself and others accountable for the published and informal values of your organization?

Managing by commitment requires that you model, by your communications and actions, making and meeting commitments. Do you?

As my daddy used to say, "We judge ourselves by our intentions; others judge us by our actions."

Importance (1–5) ____

Next Actions

NOTES

KNOW THEIR BUSINESS

PHYSICAL
WORLD
BUSINESS
SCIENCE
SYSTEMS

EXCEPTIONAL LEADERS ...
Know Their Business

IN THE LEADERSHIP MASTERY MAP®, the lower right quadrant (the exterior objective world) is where leaders focus most of their time. This part of the model represents the factual side of the business or scientific realities. Economics, systems, commercial and business aspects reside in this perspective. This is where the greatest majority of business conversations take place and rightly so. Most of us focus on the objective world in order to achieve payoffs, such as material success, money, or environmental well-being.

However, focusing on this quadrant exclusively, without taking the other three into consideration, can limit one's view. Exceptional leaders consider all four quadrants when making decisions and evaluations.

THOUGHT-PROVOKER

- Do you have a full grasp of the objective realities of the business situation you are in?
- Can you achieve the business results necessary for success?
- Do you recognize how your worldview (upper left quadrant) influences how you see a particular situation?
- Can you make the distinction between fact and subjective assessment?

Exceptional leaders achieve outstanding business and organizational results by attending to all four quadrants.

Importance (1–5)   ____

Next Actions

EXCEPTIONAL LEADERS ...
Conduct Effective Meetings

MEETINGS ARE A VERY EFFECTIVE communication tool for managing others. That said, most people would agree that ineffective meetings lose millions of dollars in productivity every day.

Recent data show that professionals spend nearly three hours per day in business meetings, and more than a third of those polled say the meetings are unproductive.

Exceptional leaders know that having too few meetings will likely result in poor communication, while having too many meetings may result in a loss of productivity. There needs to be a balance, and leaders should conduct all meetings with optimal efficiency and respect for others' time.

THOUGHT-PROVOKER

- Do you publish an agenda or set an agenda at the beginning of each meeting?
- Do you list agenda items and assign time for each?
- Are the purposes and desired outcomes unambiguous?
- Do you clearly define next action steps and assignments?
- Do you take valuable time communicating information that could be transmitted by other means?
- Do you recognize differences in individuals' tolerance for meetings and allow attendees to leave when they no longer see value in staying, so they can be more productive?

If you want to dramatically improve the productivity of your organization, improve meetings.

Importance (1–5) ____

Next Actions

EXCEPTIONAL LEADERS ...
Cultivate Potential Leaders

AN INCREASING NUMBER OF MEN AND WOMEN IN middle management resist the next step up in their careers because the corporate ladder is not as appealing as it once was, and the price of the climb is too high. For them, the sacrifices in their personal lives are too great.

Instead, they redefine how they contribute to their organizations on their own terms. Rather than subscribe to the "onward and upward" motto, these managers are more interested in life balance than in following an upward path that someone else has set.

With the high cost of turnover (upward of 300 percent of a position's annual salary) and the requirement for succession planning, leaders need to develop strategies to identify and nurture willing high-potential candidates. They also need to create environments in which leadership roles are attractive, where sacrifices to ensure success are worthwhile.

THOUGHT-PROVOKER

- Do you afford employees the flexibility to maintain work-life balance, such as flexible work schedules, at-home workdays, and educational sabbaticals?
- Does your organization have a culture that recognizes the importance of employees' families and makes accommodations in the nature of their work, such as role, location, and schedule?
- Do you have ways to identify those with the ambition to move up into leadership roles within the organization?
- Do you have a program that helps employees to look deeply at their career development desires and identify what is important to them?

In today's world, employees call the shots based on their own needs, rather than sacrifice their needs for the corporation. Exceptional leaders need to recognize this and make adjustments so the situation has a win-win outcome for all.

Importance (1–5)   _____

Next Actions

EXCEPTIONAL LEADERS ...
Develop Future Leaders

EXCEPTIONAL LEADERS ENSURE that their organizations have "bench strength" by recruiting and developing the next generation of leaders. They know that there will always be change. Businesses grow. Baby Boomers retire. The need for new leaders will always be just around the corner.

In fact, many firms are experiencing a leadership gap today. Is yours?

Today's demographics suggest that without succession plans and leadership development programs, many firms will not survive. Legacies will be lost.

Developing future leaders is a process not an event. It requires a consistent focus of attention over a period of years. Leadership development requires a written plan, milestones, and monitoring to ensure that, when the time comes for a transition, leaders are ready to carry the organization forward.

THOUGHT-PROVOKER

- Do you have a plan for developing future leaders?
- Have you determined the important characteristics of future leaders for your organization? Are you measuring those characteristics as you select, recruit, and develop employees?
- Are you building a pool of candidates?
- Are you bringing your potential leaders on board early?
- Are you supporting them as they take on challenging assignments?
- Do you reward and motivate your high potential candidates and give them future paths that will attract them?
- Have you analyzed your leadership requirements for the next 5 years, 10 years, or 20 years?
- What are the consequences of not taking the time to focus your energies on this important area?

Exceptional leaders create legacy by developing the next generation of leaders.

Importance (1–5)   _____

Next Actions

EXCEPTIONAL LEADERS ...
Do What Works

EXCEPTIONAL LEADERS ARE practical. They focus more on doing what works than on theory. This does not mean that theory is bad. After reading the latest book and hearing the current expert, a leader may certainly experiment and try new things.

However, theories must constantly be tested to ensure that they yield practical, measurable results. The implementation of unproven approaches holds substantial risk, which is particularly true with technology. Early adopters of the latest technology sometimes pay a high price for being leading-edge. Unproven systems can fail in the implementation stage. This provides rich opportunities for consultants to fix the mistakes of others.

Like so many things, there needs to be a balance between being innovative and being conservative.

THOUGHT-PROVOKER

- Do you balance innovation—trying new approaches and theories—while evaluating what really works?
- Have you invested in unproven systems, expecting spectacular results? Is it time to cut your losses?
- Perhaps you should persist with the latest innovations, such as a new system, with the expectation that it will prove out.
- Test implementation at milestones in order to ensure that things actually deliver as claimed.

Innovation is essential. Innovation that works is critical. Ask the conservative heart surgeon who prefers to use the tried and true methods until the latest and greatest innovation has proven it works.

Importance (1–5) _____

Next Actions

EXCEPTIONAL LEADERS ...
Focus on Customer Care

IN ORDER TO HAVE LOYALTY, customers must sense that the company cares about them.

We feel like Amazon cares about their customers. We continue to be loyal because, in our experience, Amazon has been consistently outstanding in its service and systems over several years. We feel that our Lexus dealership cares about us because the people there demonstrate a complete dedication to customer service in every way.

Customer service and technical service personnel must establish rapport with customers quickly, whether in person or on the phone. They must also have all the tools and systems to do their job for the customer.

Exceptional leaders know that one negative experience can cause an organization to lose a customer forever. Leaders must ensure that their organization is seen as caring about its customers and that all personnel and systems consistently demonstrate that care.

THOUGHT-PROVOKER

- Do you really care about customers?
- Do you consistently convey this to your employees and your customers?
- Do you train and check on employees to ensure that they consistently demonstrate that they care about customers?
- Do you communicate with customers formally through surveys and focus groups, as well as informally, to gauge the degree to which your organization demonstrates that it cares?

Exceptional leaders care about their customers. They constantly ensure that their customers, whether internal or external, have positive experiences every time they relate to the organization.

Importance (1–5) ____

Next Actions

EXCEPTIONAL LEADERS ...
Focus on Metrics

MEASUREMENT IS THE LANGUAGE of business. Progress toward success needs to be measured quantitatively. The Global Positioning System (GPS) provides a good analogy. This system can tell you where you have been, where you are right now, and help you measure your progress toward a goal—all through numeric measurements.

Businesses need to have their own internal GPS system. Financials—such as production figures, advertising response, sales data, customer and employee survey data, and industry-specific data—are just the beginning. Many oil field service companies, for example, can measure all of the current data for their global drilling operations through the Internet.

Determine the top dozen metrics that will measure successful progress toward your organization's goals. Many executives use charts and graphs to see the big picture and track emerging trends.

THOUGHT-PROVOKER

- Do you have a full understanding of what is really going on in your business?
- Are you immersed in numbers without really knowing what is going on?
- Do your metrics focus on the past?
- Have you determined the key metrics that, when measured frequently, will give you vital information necessary for responsive and quick decisions in a changing environment?
- What systems and personnel do you need to ensure that you get the right data?

Exceptional leaders clearly understand what is happening in the present by using metrics.

Importance (1–5)   _____

Next Actions

EXCEPTIONAL LEADERS ...
Identify the Critical Success Factor

IN A SPEECH, Larry Kellner, former CEO of Continental Airlines, stated that one of the leading reasons for Continental's financial turnaround was the ability of all employees to focus on one key performance indicator: [9] the on-time arrival of aircraft. This key indicator impacted many other indices, such as lost baggage and customer satisfaction. Continental reduced the very complex process of running an airline into one simple idea and focused on doing it well, and in the process beat the industry in on-time arrivals. [9]

In his book *Good to Great,* Jim Collins refers to the Hedgehog Concept.[10] This concept includes simply identifying what you are passionate about, what you can be the best in the world at, and what drives your economic engine. The confluence of these factors leads to incredible success.

THOUGHT-PROVOKER

- What are you and your colleagues really passionate about?
- Do you know the one big thing that you do well?
- What is the key activity that drives your economic success? Are you focusing on it?
- Do you have a culture that allows you to openly discuss the critical success factor and to focus everyone's attention on it? Continental gives a monthly payment to every employee when the company meets its on time performance objectives.

Exceptional leaders identify the one factor beyond all others that creates success for their company and they focus on it relentlessly.

Importance (1–5)   ____

Next Actions

EXCEPTIONAL LEADERS ...
Keep Their Key Employees

EXCEPTIONAL LEADERS KNOW that the loss of critical employees can deal a significant blow to an organization. In a robust economy, companies are more vulnerable to turnover. Even in a slowing economy there can still be shortages in key areas.

Ambitious people need to feel that they are valued. They need to be challenged, appreciated, rewarded, and respected. Exceptional leaders ensure that these needs are met.

Most resignations come from dissatisfaction with a boss, the culture, the job, career progress, or, on occasion, inequitable compensation.

Exceptional leaders remain alert to sources of satisfaction and dissatisfaction among their employees. They take the necessary initiatives to make changes when needed and to continually market the value of working for the organization.

THOUGHT-PROVOKER

- Do you continuously promote your employment brand both internally and externally, emphasizing the value of being a part of your organization?
- Are you and other leaders in the organization sufficiently close to your employees to know their level of job satisfaction?
- Do you have a feedback system in place to measure the degree of employee satisfaction, such as employee engagement/satisfaction surveys?
- Are your employees proud to work for your organization?
- Do your managers treat employees with respect?
- Does your culture foster a sense of belonging and opportunity?

Exceptional leaders create employment loyalty by providing employees with a great place to work and opportunities for career growth.

Importance (1–5) ____

Next Actions

EXCEPTIONAL LEADERS ...
Set Up Customer Friendly Systems

WE ALL KNOW that the customer is king. Exceptional leaders know that the systems set up to interface with customers must create a positive experience. These systems include phone answering systems, and the Internet. Customers must know that these systems are designed to enhance service rather than simply to save the company money.

A good example lies in the convenience of purchasing airline tickets online and printing boarding passes. This practice saves the company money, and it also enhances the customer's experience and saves them time.

Answering systems and voicemail must do the same. Customers must experience convenience and ease in getting to the right person and discovering information in a timely manner.

Sometimes systems that are set up to reduce costs do not enhance the customer experience, creating significant customer dissatisfaction, while potentially saving the company money only in the short run.

Do you really believe that the delay in a customer service department's phone system is that they are "temporarily experiencing a high call volume due to demand for our products," or have they just reduced staff?

THOUGHT-PROVOKER

- Do you challenge your staff to ensure that all customer interface systems function optimally?
- Is the automated directory simple, quick, and easy to understand?
- Does the caller get to the right person every time?
- Do customers have a positive experien all of the time?
- Do you test your Web site and online ordering system regularly so bugs can be fixed and navigation made as easy as possible?
- Do you have a flawless system to respond to online inquiries in an accurate and timely manner?

Exceptional leaders ensure that their customers, both internal and external, have a positive experience every time.

Importance in my work (1–5) _____

Next Actions

THESE ARE THE TOP FIVE THINGS
THAT I WILL WORK ON.

_____

_____

_____

_____

_____

_____

To buy copies of this book go to
www.thinkingpartners.com

Bibliography

1. Wilber, Ken. *A Theory of Everything: An Integral Vision for Business, Politics, Science and Spirituality*. Boston: Shambhala, 2001.
2. Stockdale, James. *A Vietnam Experience: Ten Years of Reflection*. Stanford: Hoover   Institution, 1984.
3. Drucker, Peter F. *The Essential Drucker: The Best of Sixty Years of Peter Drucker's Essential Writings on Management*. New York: Collins, 2003.
4. Freedman, Lucy D., and Lisa J. Marshall. *Smart Work*. Dubuque: Kendall Hunt, 2003.
5. Scott, Cynthia D., and Denise T. Jaffe. *Managing Change at Work: Leading People Through Organizational Transitions, Revised Edition*. Ithaca, NY: Crisp Publications, 1995.
6. Welch, Jack, and Suzy Welch. *Winning*. New York: Collins, 2005.
7. Watzlawick, Paul. *The Language of Change: Elements of Therapeutic Communication*. New   York: W. W. Norton & Company, 1993.
8. *Gallup, Inc. "Gallup Study: Engaged Employees Inspire Company Innovation." Gallup   Management Journal (October 12, 2006),*
9. Kellner, Larry, "Continental Airlines Success Factors." Speech, Houston Strategic Forum, Houston, TX, October 27, 2006.
10. Collins, Jim. *Good to Great: Why Some Companies Make the Leap ... and Others Don't,   First Edition*. New York: Collins, 2001.
11. Goleman, Daniel, Richard E. Boyatzis, and Annie McKee. *Primal Leadership: Learning to Lead with Emotional Intelligence*. Boston: Harvard Business School, 2004.

CPSIA information can be obtained
at www.ICGtesting.com
Printed in the USA
LVHW081916040119
602630LV00030B/701/P

9 781484 916650